FRIEND OF ACPL

women's groups

Sparkling

**DO NOT REMOVE
CARDS FROM POCKET**

ALLEN COUNTY PUBLIC LIBRARY

FORT WAYNE, INDIANA 46802

You may return this book to any agency, branch,
or bookmobile of the Allen County Public Library

DEMCO

Sparkling Devotions for Women's Groups

Mary A. Vanderney

BAKER BOOK HOUSE
Grand Rapids, Michigan 49506

Copyright 1985 by
Baker Book House Company

ISBN: 0-8010-9300-7

Second printing, January 1987

Printed in the United States of America

Contents

    Foreword vii
1 What Is the World Coming To? 1
2 The Good-for-nothing Tree 4
3 After House Guests Have Gone 8
4 Run Away to Pray 11
5 Aunt Hildy, a Model 14
6 Mouse Troubles 18
7 Instant Happiness 21
8 Getting Unstuck 24
9 Do I Ask the Sunset Why? 27
10 The International Birthday Party 30
11 Sunset? Sunrise? 34
12 Lights 37
13 Why? 40
14 The Do-nothing Day 44
15 The Kettle Huggers 47
16 Push that Button Again 50
17 The Negatives and the Positives 53
18 Grandmother's Personal Progress Report 57
19 What's Wrong with a Happy Day? 60
20 Selves 63

21 A Day for God to Laugh   67
22 What Is Bread?   71
23 I Remember Them Well   74
24 Times My Father Took Off for Chicago   78
25 Boy's Eye-view of His Country   81
26 Emergency Run   84
27 When Charity and Gratitude Become Acquainted   87
28 Don't Play in the Street   91
29 Harrison's Short Successful Life   95
30 Whose Child Is This?   98
31 The Policeman's Prayer   102
32 What If Parents Had Never Met?   105
33 Relativities   108
34 Is Your Slogan "IAK?"   111
35 Jean's Upside-down Life   115

Foreword

"If only I had a better understanding of myself and of others!" How many times we have made that remark; how many times we have heard it. All of us who strive to be stronger, better individuals, finding our paths in what we believe to be the Christian life, are *always* working for inner spiritual growth and always, always sensing our continuing need for it. We want to feel the heat of the fire of knowing we are progressing in our Christian lives. We say often, too often, we believe, "I should have known better. I should have better understood my neighbor, my friend, my relative. Why can't I remember the teachings of Jesus?"

However, when we are at times tuned in to matters of the Spirit, his inner voice takes control of our thoughts and we have insight into the needs of others, even of ourselves. We are forever better human beings for having had this experience. We say, as did the little boy after an exciting art class, "I'll never be the same again!"

But is every facet of our lives completely satisfying after one insight? No. Each day brings its own particular challenging situations. We need constructive methods of dealing with them. We need to deal with our own moods and emotions as well as with other people. We pray earnestly and then move ahead, knowing we have the support of our heavenly Father.

Sometimes the growth comes like a shooting star, emblazoning our lives. At other times, the growth is simply ground out of us like so much meal. Even so, what elation we feel as we achieve one small step in understanding ourselves, our families, friends and strangers. In triumph we cry, "Thank you, God!"

Then there is always tomorrow and tomorrow. We are eager for the new experiences, or if we are tired, not so eager.

Occasionally, we pause for a look back down the mountain trail we have climbed. There we see the steppingstones we have crossed in order to reach our present level of learning and living the joys, sorrows, laughter, tears, lessons with new understanding.

The chapters of this book, with related Scripture texts and prayers, emerged from my own efforts and those of friends, relatives, and often strangers in propelling my journey toward a richer Christian life. They are the distillation of my own thinking and of those about me, an affirmation of guidance for each day.

"As I approach this day, I shall meet it with open eyes, with open ears, and with an open mind. This will prepare me to see and hear and try to understand all that God places in my path. If I am consciously aware of new experiences and receptive to their lessons, if I try to keep an open mind and an understanding heart, God will be my guide." This determination has opened to me the fresh look at my life I offer you in this book.

As you read and share these thoughts with other women may each of you find inspiration, courage, even joy, in facing your particular problems and encounters. May you become increasingly aware, too, that no matter how many steps upward into this higher consciousness we wish to go, there are always more steps to be taken, more steppingstones to cross. A journey is much more than one step.

But, in moments of reflection and assessment while you pause for a momentary backward look, you will say, "With God's help, love, and care, I *have* moved many more steps along the Divinely-led path of living."

Mary Vandermey

1

What Is the World Coming To?

The heart of the wise teacheth his mouth, and addeth learning to his lips (Prov. 16:23).

A wise man will hear, and will increase learning; and a man of understanding shall attain unto wise counsels (Prov. 1:5).

Judge not according to the appearance, but judge righteous judgment (John 7:24).

I wish everyone having negative thoughts about teenagers could have been with me one evening at the shopping mall. I learned *whom* the world is coming to.

I had errands to do at the mall, but believe I was divinely

guided to make the journey. It was up to me to look, to see, and to have a change of heart.

First, however, my own negative thoughts about teenagers were strengthened on my way to the mall when a youngster on a motorbike cut in front of me, swinging recklessly as only they seem capable of doing. I swerved to avoid hitting him and consequently bumped into the curb. With my heart thumping, I exclaimed to no one particular, "What is the world coming to, anyway?"

I found the answer at the mall, which was filled with crowds viewing displays of works by high school students. Fascinated, I strolled from one exhibit to another. As I went along I began to have a softening of my heart, a tenderness in my mind.

Paintings in oils, acrylics and watercolors attracted me first. What sensitivity to and skill in blending colors had created the effects. How delicate were the flower scenes; how majestic and strong the mountain scenes. What insights and loving care were evident in the charcoal sketch of an aged man; the lines in the face literally pulled the character from beneath the flesh. The teenaged artists stood proudly beside their works, chatting happily with viewers.

Next, I found tables and standing displays of exquisitely tailored slacks and shirts, of delicate blouses and skirts embroidered with roses and hyacinths. I saw a patchwork quilt in the pine cone pattern and was reminded of my great-grandmother's handiwork.

Farther on, I stood entranced by a display of woodcarvings of expertly cut forms and details, and ceramics rivaling pieces I had seen in Mexico.

On I went, occasionally moving aside to make way for teenagers pushing senior citizens in wheelchairs.

The science display was beyond my comprehension. Levers moved up and down in steady rhythm. Windmills powered fans. At a minilab, white-coated teenagers poured liquids into test tubes and watched the liquids turn red, green or yellow, all done with serious intent and professional attitudes.

Now to the cookery. Boys and girls made breads by carefully measuring ingredients, using a bread-mixing machine, shaping the loaves into pans, allowing them to rise, then thrusting them into ready portable ovens. These teenagers, too, went about their business with dignity and efficiency.

My mental pictures went beyond the present scenes to the adults who had faith in these teenagers. Parents, teachers, ministers, and friends had patience and understanding, and had inspired the children to live full creative lives. I was proud and grateful to those parents, teachers, and youth leaders who are often accused of not caring. They do care. It was evident in this place. I felt contrition for myself and my previous attitude toward members of the upcoming generation. After all, what had I done to inspire them?

But I was proud, too, of these teenagers as I watched them at work. I now knew the answer to my question, "What is the world coming to?" It is coming to such teenagers as I saw at the mall. The world will be a better, safer place because they live in it and accomplish what they do.

Lord, may I this day praise rather than condemn. May I inspire someone to make positive, creative use of his time and talents to advance science or beauty for all the world to inherit and enjoy. Above all, thank you for youth dedicated to making this world a finer, more loving place for us all. Amen.

2

The Good-for-nothing Tree

Lo, they have rejected the word of the Lord; and what wisdom is in them? (Jer. 8:9).

Let us choose to us judgment: let us know among ourselves what is good (Job 34:4).

God saw every thing that he had made, and, behold, it was very good (Gen. 1:31).

For years we resented the maple tree growing at the west side of the house. What good was it?

Each spring it grew fresh leaves and a crop of arils, the winged product for which we could see no earthly use, unless for the purpose of making us labor by raking them into the litter box. That maple tree dropped leaves all summer. In autumn it sprayed the grass with masses of paper-like pieces of red and yellow, basketfuls of which went into the litterbox. How the rubbish men must have resented the added loads!

Every year we said, "That tree must go!" What good was it? Had God made a mistake when he created such trees? There they were, producing no fruit, making messes of our manicured lawns, and during the winters, standing stark naked.

Anna, my neighbor, retired from her work in a home for abandoned children, often came in for morning coffee after my family had departed. Together we wondered about that useless tree. "We must cut it down, we must cut it down," I told her in a litany that accomplished nothing.

It is said progress and insight come when we have grown wise enough to receive it. I must have been wise enough to receive it one particular morning. I lingered over coffee and reveled in the quiet of the house that followed the confusion of my family's morning departure. I stared at the maple tree, resenting it as usual. It was winter and the tree was bare.

Anna came in and voiced her growing discontent. "What good am I now? I have no children, no husband. I've lived a useless life, just like that tree you are always complaining about."

I murmured the usual words of comfort, but she only sipped the coffee I had poured for her.

My glance returned to the window and the maple tree. Something new had appeared. A bluejay had alighted on a lower branch. He flicked his tail and turned his head this way and that. Then he began to fly about in a crazy pattern, going so fast he seemed to be propelled by a motor. Round and round the bird went. I held my breath lest he smash headlong into a branch and knock himself out. I wanted to cry, "You'll break a wing, you'll break a leg!"

But the jay did none of those things. His morning calisthenics finished, he soared away to tend to the rest of his day's activities.

"Well," I commented to Anna, staring dourly at the wintry

scene, "that tree is good for something. It's an exercise pen for a bluejay!"

I began to muse on the maple tree. I noticed, for the first time, several empty nests in the crotches of the branches. How many birds had nested in the shelter of the tree when its leaves were full? How many nestlings had hatched and grown there before flying away to be on their own? My mind stretched further. I heard the shouts of the little children as they sailed higher and higher in the swing anchored on a maple tree branch. I remembered how much shade that tree had given our home on hot summer days, and how often Grandfather had pulled out his chair to cool himself in its shade and the summer breeze.

I told Anna of this discovery, but she was silent.

In my mind I said, "Oh, maple tree, I apologize. You are good for something. I'm sorry we verbally abused you. You knew your business, your usefulness. You knew God placed you here for the use we made of you, and you went on fulfilling your destiny."

I turned to Anna. "Anna, that tree has been good for many things. Think of yourself as being like that tree. How many little children you have nursed, how many dripping noses you have wiped, how many cut fingers you have bandaged, how many little ones you have given love. Oh, Anna, you have fulfilled God's purpose in making you, just as that tree has. Think how many babies might never have known the warmth and love of a mother's breast if it hadn't been for you. Appreciate yourself, Anna. Warm your heart with the memories of your worthiness."

Anna stared at the tree awhile and watched another bird come, alight on a branch, and soar away. She pushed aside the coffee cup. Tears came to her eyes.

"Yes, yes. It has not been for nothing. It has not been for nothing."

I gave her a tissue and she wiped her eyes. She rose from the table, went to the door, and opened it. She went outside, and just before the door closed I heard her crooning a lullaby.

Thank you, Lord, for all creation. You knew what you were doing in creating everything, from trees to humans. Our full appreciation of your work often comes to us late, but we are grateful nevertheless. We are grateful for the food we take for granted and the beauty we do not always see. We thank you for fragrances and shade, and for the warmth and love of people like Anna. Thank you for the maple trees of our lives. Amen.

3

After House Guests Have Gone

Peace, peace to him that is far off, and to him that is near, saith the Lord (Isa. 57:19).

Ointment and perfume rejoice the heart: so doth the sweetness of a man's friend by hearty counsel (Prov. 27:9).

Now the Lord of peace himself give you peace always by all means (2 Thess. 3:16).

How I had anticipated having old friends come from Arizona for a three-day visit. We had not seen each other since school days.

We went sightseeing, and I saw more of our area than I had

ever seen. Evenings we talked. "Do you remember . . . ? What ever happened to . . . ? How is . . . ?" We relived school days. We talked of our plans, our pleasures, our sorrows, our special blessings.

In early morning my guests were gone. The silence seemed to scream, "They're gone, they're gone!" Bedclothes lay rumpled, waiting to be washed and stored. Breakfast dishes from the hurried meal littered the counter. An empty sadness filled the house.

Left alone with this emptiness I could not even say, "Thank you, Lord, for dear friends." I could not say, "Thanks for work to do." Standing in the still house, I thought, "The departure of loved ones is like a small death. The house is like a tomb from which even ghosts have fled." The foggy morning did me no good.

But eventually I mustered courage, which we all do to survive the necessary routines of our lives. I changed the beds and reveled in the fragrance of softening agent lingering in the creases of the sheets. I fluffed the pillows and found myself saying, "Thank you for the cotton that grew so these sheets could be made. Thank you for the polyester pillows. Thank you for the trees that grew to be made into this furniture."

In the kitchen I enjoyed the clatter of dishes in the sink. Later, the humming of the vacuum cleaner was like symphonic music, for when spirits soar, all is music. I was grateful for a plane droning overhead, and for the neighbor's barking dog, which ordinarily irritated me. The indoor and outdoor sounds began to fill the emptiness I had been experiencing.

The doorbell rang. It was a door-to-door salesman. I was able to wish him a happy day while telling him I had no need for his wares, in spite of his assurances my life would be richer and easier if I paid the outrageous price.

I went into the garden to pluck the weeds that had taken advantage of me during the company time. I washed the bed linens and extra towels, enjoying the clean smell of detergents.

At last the house and garden were in order. Mentally, I was in order too.

I went back over the day's events. Not only had I been grateful for my friends, but I also gained an increasing appreciation of the common things that make up life: the plants, the household, the dishes, the sounds, ears with which to hear, and eyes with which to see. I was back to normal.

Lord, thank you for old friends who come back into our lives, and for tasks to fill the vacuum their departures create. Thank you for strength, health, the will to pick up our sagging spirits, and the ability to move back into our routines after disruptions. Amen.

4

Run Away to Pray

When thou prayest, enter into thy closet, and when thou hast shut thy door, pray to thy Father which is in secret; and thy Father which seeth in secret shall reward thee openly (Matt. 6:6).

I will pray with the spirit, and I will pray with the understanding also (1 Cor. 14:15).

Your Father knoweth what things ye have need of, before ye ask him (Matt. 6:8).

Today I ran away from home.

I'm certain the Lord watched me as I went. I undoubtedly had his approval. He saw me torn between two alternatives, alternatives that might well change the course of my life.

Should I do this, or that? I'm sure he watched me as I became frustrated by indecision. He knew how I am irked by everyday trivia while I attempt to deal with greater problems.

I prayed for guidance. Nothing happened. Finally, I cried to myself, "Let me out of here!"

Without further thought, I dressed and got into the car. I entered the freeway, free of my usual shaking and dread, a major accomplishment for me. Generally, I try to figure out ways to avoid the freeway.

Happily, I left the heavy traffic behind me at the three cities I passed, and I was on my way to the open spaces. I sailed through the pass where sun-bleached desert mountains loomed to the right, to the left, and ahead of me. Spikes of cacti stood like sentinels. I imagined them staring pityingly at me. Me, with my problems! They seem to have none. They grow whether or not it rains, and are seldom disturbed by humans because of their sharp prongs with which they protect themselves.

Rocks jutted from the sand dunes I passed. Wind beat against my little car, and the wind whipped by passing trailer-trucks made it shudder. I opened the windows to let the dry desert wind beat against my face. I breathed deeply, and regeneration began taking place in my body and mind. I had left my troublsome indecision behind.

I reached a desert outpost and stopped at a little cafe. A half dozen trucks parked nearby indicated the food would be simple but excellent.

The waitress kept up a chatter with the truck drivers. She called them pal and friend. She asked me, "What'll it be, friend?" Friend. How heartwarming, even though good for business. The sandwich and coffee were exactly right.

I went out into the hot wind again, not minding that my hair quickly looked like a ragged broom. The bright sun warmed me to the bone. I had forgotten about the decision I must make. Instead, I simply gave myself entirely to the deliciousness of living.

I went into a store specializing in dates, nuts, raisins and dried exotic fruits—fruits of the desert. I bought a supply, paying more than I would have at home.

I sat in a little park and watched children, brown as Arabs, playing. I pushed their swings, and my ears soaked up their laughter. When I left, they cried, "Come again. We love you!"

Now the bright sun was a crown over the mountains to the west. I drove home, leaving the windows open. The wind had changed to desert-night cold. Never mind.

Home welcomed me with open arms, as though I had been to a far country.

I sat down trying to review the day. But it was now a memory, a lapse in time. I mentally picked up the decison I must make. Suddenly, I knew, I knew! It had been made for me.

I now know I went to the desert to pray. I had needed refreshment, relaxation, a glimpse of the glory of creation. Oh, I did not pray consciously. But somehow in appreciating sun, wind, sky, and sand, I had prayed for guidance. I prayed and let go of my problem, giving it over to God. My reward: knowing which way to go.

A walk along the street in the rain might have brought my solution. An afternoon in the park listening to children playing could have done it. But it was the getting away that made it possible to pray without stress.

Lord, thank you for giving us the wisdom to sometimes put space between ourselves and our problems. In this way we clear our minds and open them so you can freely enter our consciousness. Thank you for havens to which we may go to think. Thank you for giving us the right answers. Amen.

5

Aunt Hildy, a Model

No good thing will he withhold from them that walk uprightly (Ps. 84:11).

Love one another with a pure heart fervently (1 Peter 1:22).

He that loveth his brother abideth in the light, and there is none occasion of stumbling in him (1 John 2:10).

Aunt Hildy, as she is known throughout the neighborhood, is being imposed upon. Everyone tells her so, and has been telling her for years: the people next door, the people across the street, and her son Tom, who lives far away.

Aunt Hildy hears, but she does not listen. She goes about

living her life with a fierce but smiling intent. The tight bun of gray hair at her neck bobs up and down mornings. But by nightfall it hangs loosely, tired, no doubt, from all it's been through that day. But Aunt Hildy is as bouncy at nightfall as in the morning.

The reason everyone tells Aunt Hildy she is being imposed upon is the constant stream of widowers and bachelors wearing a path in the cement walk to her house. These gentle, helpless men bring Hildy their laundry and their ripped seams. They also bring their mental agonies and problems.

The neighborhood children are in the act, too. They bring Hildy robins with injured wings or dogs with wild oat heads lodged between inflamed toes, plus their own cut fingers. They have been known to bring bikes with flat tires. Hildy has all the medications and equipment necessary for performing first aid in such emergencies. But for mending injured egos she quotes the Bible by chapter and verse to fit the occasion.

Hildy, doing the laundry and ironing, has the radio going full blast, and sings along with the music. If you protest too vehemently that she is being imposed upon, that she is overdoing, she says cheerfully, "I like the smell of clean clothes drying on the line. I like to help an injured bird. I like to listen to someone telling the story of his pain, not because I like to see anyone hurt, but because I know the telling eases the pain. And he knows I won't tell anyone else. It makes me thankful the Lord has given me this good health."

If we talk too much about the parade of injured birds and dogs, Hildy's blue eyes blaze. If we tell her the children's parents should be doing their duty, Hildy says, "I don't know their problems. But I do know if God hadn't intended for me to do this work for his creatures, he'd have sent someone else." Oh, Hildy knows exactly what the Lord intended her to do!

So year after year, the bachelors and widowers go home with their clothing clean and mended and their mental pains eased. The baby birds' rescuers release them, and Hildy watches with the children as the birds fly away with happy chirps.

One day a child protested, "He didn't even say thank you!"

Hildy replied, "If you hear his song, you know he's grateful. There are lots of ways to say thanks."

Holidays arrive. Hildy invites her heterogeneous family for dinner. Do the guests help with expenses? No, for Aunt Hildy flatly refuses to let a guest pay. Of course, she graciously accepts their gifts of flowers, candy, and silk scarves. But she has privately told each guest that her Social Security checks and quarterly interest from a small investment provide her enough money. Finally, she says, "Jesus blessed the few loaves and fishes and look what happened! I bless my income." The gray bun bobs for emphasis.

One day Aunt Hildy had an accident. She broke her right arm, falling from an elm tree she was climbing to rescue one of God's creatures. She said it was God's though some neighbors said the bird was the responsibility of an irresponsible mother bird.

Hildy landed in the hospital.

Who came to help out, even before the neighbors finished shaking their heads over the impossibility of changing Hildy? The bachelors, the widowers and the children came. They came in ones, twos and threes or more. They mowed and sprinkled the lawn, washed the neglected windows, and swept the drive.

They visited the hospital in such droves the staff clamped down on the numbers of visitors and floral arrangements permitted in Hildy's room. Little Freddy managed to slip in with an injured toad for Hildy to mend. What a stir that made on the third floor! Nurses, aides, doctors, and maintenance men got into the act of shooing out Freddy and the reptilian patient.

Aunt Hildy, likely the first time in her life, had a temper outburst. "That creature needs attention the same as people. We all belong to the Lord. We help each other, even the little creatures. What better place than a hospital for helping?"

Hildy's arm mended, and one day she went home. Now she is back doing the Lord's work and being a model of Christian living.

Wouldn't we all like to be a little more like Aunt Hildy?

Lord, we can't all be Aunt Hildys. But we can take time to help some person in need, to reply sympathetically to a troubled person's story, to speak with the lonely ones. Make us aware of these needs, and give us the urge to respond. Thank you for the Aunt Hildys who touch our lives. Amen.

6

Mouse Troubles

As ye would that men should do to you, do ye also to them likewise (Luke 6:31).

If a man be overtaken in a fault, ye which are spiritual, restore such an one in the spirit of meekness; considering thyself, lest thou also be tempted (Gal. 6:1).

Man looketh on the outward appearance, but the Lord looketh on the heart (1 Sam. 16:7).

One day I resolved to tell off someone who had, I believed, deliberately humiliated me. I fretted and fumed. How could she criticize me for handling the church bazaar the way I did? And before all the club members!

Basically, I know all this fretting harms me more than the other person. I know that a Christian should turn the other cheek—which means to let it go in one ear and out the other. But I am often frail of mind.

So for a time I continued plotting. "I will rise at the next club meeting and resign from the club. Let her run everything!"

Oh, the holiness of the injured party!

My scheming mind wouldn't let me sleep. I prayed, "Forgive me for having vengeful thoughts." But she had no right! "Patience," I then told myself. "The answer will come, the right answer. You will then understand what you must do."

The answer did come through this delightful English story.

A certain gentleman's house was being remodelled. He could not live in it during the process, so he moved to a nearby motel. All he brought with him was a box containing his shaving kit and two pairs of socks.

The clerk asked the gentleman for his baggage before showing him to his room. The gentleman did not think it strange that he had brought no baggage. After all, he could go home each day for a change of clothing.

During the night the man heard strange noises, the patter of little feet. He turned on the light. A mouse scurried across the carpet and under the telly.

Disturbed, the gentleman complained to the maid the next morning.

She shook her head in disbelief. "Mr. Robbins would never harbor mice. He would not tolerate them."

The guest became more disturbed. He *had* seen a mouse. He told the story to the gardener, who was busy pruning roses.

The man shook his head in disbelief. "Oh, no, sir. Impossible. Mr. Robbins runs a clean place. A first-class place."

The complaint was noised about. Mr. Robbins himself spoke to the guest. "Sir, I hear you complained of a mouse in your room. I differ with you. There are no mice here."

The gentleman continued to live in the motel because it was convenient to his home. The mouse continued its nightly visits. The man felt more and more put upon. Finally, he bought a mousetrap, a cage-like contraption. "I'll show them!" he vowed, and baited the trap with cheese. He would prove he was right.

Next morning the mouse was in the trap. Now the man could show them all! But as he picked up the cage, a shattering thought struck him. "Isn't this ridiculuous! Here I am, a grown man. How can I degrade myself this way? I am larger than a mere mouse. I have always prided myself in being a Christian, yet I use a harmless creature, one of God's creatures, to prove I am right. I have my faults, too."

Shame overtook him. "Am I better than they? After all, what must they think of me? I came here with a box, one box, having a shaving kit and two pairs of socks. How strange they must think I am."

Quickly he took the mouse outside, and under the shelter of the hedge, released it. He walked taller when he left the motel, triumphant in his new understanding.

The solution to my problem of the critical person? I did not speak my mind to my supposed enemy. I understood that we all have our own opinions and perceptions of situations, and we are entitled to them. Tolerance of our differences was my key to letting the matter rest.

Kind Father, help me forgive others their weaknesses as I must forgive my own. With the strength of your divine presence help all of us to be less critical, and to share the world in peaceful understanding. Amen.

7

Instant Happiness

Thou has made known to me the ways of life; thou shalt make me full of joy with thy countenance (Acts 2:28).

It was meet that we should make merry, and be glad (Luke 15:32).

Out of the mouth of babes and sucklings thou hast perfected praise (Matt. 21:16).

In the shopping mall a large crowd had been attracted to a fenced-off area. People were curious about something going on there.

It proved to be a children's photography shop where a child of seven or eight months was seated in the draped, spotlighted area. He was crying as though he were in pain. Had someone stuck a pin in him?

The mother and father stood at ringside. They must be the parents; none of the other spectators had such anguished looks. There stood the photographer, also, frantically waving a fuzzy teddy bear.

What were the anxious parents, photographer, and onlookers with forced laughter asking of the child? They were seeking his instant happiness so they could record the moment for posterity.

Instant happiness. What about it?

We wonder if we could hand someone a package and say, "Here is a gift for you. It is happiness." But we know that if the person opened the package, he would find nothing.

Still, the search for happiness goes on. Parents want their children to be happy. The bride's mother wants instant and permanent happiness for her daughter. The groom wants happiness for his bride, and she wants the same for her husband. Oh, the frustration when happiness does not come, and the tension when we try to force it, as with the crying child in the mall.

What is happiness, then, and can it be acquired? Experts say that happiness is an intense feeling or emotion, which comes because we have received something we treasure or have longed for. Someone declares great affection or admiration for us, and . . . happiness!

Or, happiness is the glow we feel when we have helped a loved one or a stranger, not because we felt obligated, but because we wanted to. Happiness comes when we see the resulting flash of gratitude in the loved one's eyes. And happiness comes to the recipients of our love when we have given it freely, with no strings attached.

What does the Bible say of happiness? Actually, it equates it with contentment.

"There is nothing better for a man, than that he should eat and drink, and find enjoyment in his toil. . . . for to the man who pleases him God gives wisdom and knowledge and joy . . . ." (Eccles. 2:26). "Thou hast made known to me the ways of life; thou shalt make me full of joy with thy countenance" (Acts 2:28).

There is more to the story of the child in the mall.

The parents, the photographer, and the onlookers, who had waved scarves and purses and flags, tired in their efforts and went about their own business. The fuzzy bear lay abandoned on the counter.

Suddenly, the child saw it. He reached for it. The weary photographer picked up the bear and offered it to the child once more. The photographer did not give it in a here-take-this-and-be-happy attitude. He offered it freely.

Freely! A miracle! The child reached for the bear, a smile as bright as summer on his face. The bear belonged to him.

The alert photographer took advantage and snapped the picture. It was a moment of happiness for everyone.

Lord, we know that in your service we find our joys. Even when we often cry in sorrow or in pain, we know contentment will come again. We treasure the moments of happiness that come to us; we release them when we must, confident they will return to us at the time and in the place known to you. This we do with complete trust in you. We are grateful for your protection and promises of joy that come to us even through our clouds. Amen.

8

Getting Unstuck

Every man that striveth for mastery is temperate in all things (1 Cor. 9:25).

Put on the whole armour of God, that ye may be able to stand against the wiles of the devil (Eph. 6:11).

Surely goodness and mercy shall follow me all the days of my life (Ps. 23:6).

Monday morning. Getting organized for the week. So much to do. Letters to write. Household to set in order after weekend guests.

The phone rang. "Will you bake a cake for the church bake sale? You make such marvelous cakes." Flattery!

The phone rang again and again. "Don't forget the election

at club Tuesday night. Would you mind? Will you call these people?"

The phone rang again and again. Would I . . . ? Would I?

Now, it's beautiful to have so many calls, but that morning I didn't consider it popularity. It was plain imposition. I was being put upon. But after five minutes of that way of thinking I felt guilty, more and more guilty. "I should, I should! But I'm tired of the have-tos! Do I *have to*?"

The trouble with idealists, I decided, is that when we feel we are not living up to our potentials, if we are not having the right attitudes, we tend to fall apart. When we are disillusioned with ourselves, we hurt mentally. We become stuck on feeling sorry for ourselves.

So all morning, as I produced the promised cake, I struggled with being stuck on myself.

At noon J called and asked me to attend an Alcoholics Anonymous luncheon meeting with him. I wanted to refuse. I was still in my stuck situation. But I wanted to please J. This was my first step in becoming unstuck. When he calls, I know he is hurting and needs me.

We sat at long tables. The leader for the day called on first this person, then that one, to relate his week's triumphs and problems, if any. And who doesn't have some of both?

A man I shall call Phil went to the podium. Though I had only half listened up to this time, when Phil began to talk I snapped to attention. Here was someone with a story.

Phil said, "Thirty years ago I lost my wife, my children, my job. I lost everything I cared about because of the bottle. Then I had only the bottle to comfort me. I tried to drown my troubles, but troubles know how to swim.

"I landed in Ward B, where they dried me out. While this was going on, I recalled what my father once told me: 'Always keep an ace in the hole, Phil. You know what that ace is? It's your Lord, God. He'll pull you through.'

"Now AA says we recognize a higher power, a God as we understand him, and that we should accept him. I began to pray. Some of you came to see me way back then. You led me through the twelve steps. Let me say thank you, right now."

As Phil went on, I began to follow him sympathetically and admiringly. I thought I knew something of his hurts and needs, and of his great efforts to restore his equilibrium through his own accomplishments.

He went on, "Dried out, I went and got a job. I was paid bottom scale. That's all I was worth. But I kept praying, and kept working hard. I got off the 'poor me' kick. You know what?" He paused, smiling triumphantly. "Today I have my wife and children back. They are proud of me. I have a position, not just a job. And I am sober. Why is this so? I never stopped praying. I never stopped doing what I was supposed to do to keep sober. Finally, I didn't want a drink! I thank God!"

I went home, completely absorbed in Phil's story, the story of a man who had once been in deep trouble, but who had triumphed.

Suddenly, I knew I had become unstuck. My mind soared with the thought of what we can accomplish if we try, and if we seek that outside help. God, I decided, is the outside power who enters the innermost parts of our lives. God is the power to pull us triumphantly through our struggles. All we need say is, "I believe," and he helps. To think on him liberates us from feeling sorry for ourselves.

God, rather than fret away hours because of pressures or disappointments or low moods, may we always put to good use the time which is exclusively ours. Free us from self-pity, and let us live life for its own sake as well as for yours. Thank you for stories of triumphant lives, and make us realize that we, too, can always draw strength and determination from your love and power. Amen.

9

Do I Ask the Sunset Why?

Give me understanding, and I shall keep thy law; yea, I shall observe it with my whole heart (Ps. 119:34).

Wherein thou judgest another, thou condemnest thyself; for thou that judgest doest the same things (Rom. 2:1).

And this I pray, that your love may abound yet more and more in knowledge and in all judgment (Phil. 1:9).

I wanted my friend to be what I thought he ought to be. I asked him why he wasn't more aggressive, why he is never on time. Why, why, why? Oh, I criticized in a nice way. I was not angry, I was not loud, I was only gently persuasive. So I thought.

But I hurt his feelings. I even made him angry, though he controlled his anger. He is himself, and that's it. He will live his life. He was not stubborn, only positive.

Someone has said those we love we harm a little. I hurt my friend and I was sorry. I have no right to change those I love. Did I not love my friend before I discovered his so-called faults? And do I not expect those who love me to accept me with my faults?

Oh, I argued with myself even as a wife/husband/parent/child must struggle over similar situations. My criticism of my friend, I decided, was not from loving too much but from expecting his near perfection.

That evening I saw clearly where I had been in error. I was taught the lesson by none less than the Creator. Standing on the terrace, I watched a colorful sunset, and learned a lesson I shall not forget.

I became breathlessly in awe of the beauty of the sunset as it waved a final goodbye to the closing day. Sunstreaks and flags wafting reds, golds, pale yellows, blues, and purples all proclaimed the glory of God.

But not once did I ask, "Sunset, why don't you have more red on the north, more blue on the south? And after all, you do not need all those yellow ribbons shooting up from your center. Purple would have made for better color harmony. Why don't you have . . . ?"

No, I did not question for even a second the sunset's taste in color harmony. I accepted it in all its gloriousness, with any flaws I may have imagined. I embraced it completely, without reservation, opening loving arms and heart to this marvelous gift from the Creator.

My friend! The thought of him struck me suddenly. How might I fit myself into a pattern of letting this loved one find his own way, be his own person? How had I accepted the sunset so completely that I had no desire to change it, but rather, desired to let it be its own beautiful self?

Why, I simply yielded to it! The yielding came through a working of the Spirit on my emotions, more than through my mind. It continued with my letting go of my body tension, of relaxing muscle after muscle once the Spirit had full control.

Then did I fully accept my friend. Nothing tangible changed, but the spiritual change had loosened the mental attitude I had been maintaining. I was ready to permit my loved one, my friend, to be himself and to admire him for it.

Acceptance of persons—a prerequisite of love.

Lord, give me patience with others. Guide me away from fault finding, and let me readily allow those I love to find your way for them. Help me to support my friends and loved ones while I permit them the freedom to be the individuals you created in your image. Forgive my impatience with others and with myself. Thank you for my strength and determination for accomplishing these aims. Amen.

10

The International Birthday Party

Thou shalt open thine hand wide unto thy brother (Deut. 15:11).

Let us consider one another to provoke unto love and to good works (Heb. 10:24).

Add to your faith . . . godliness . . . brotherly kindness . . . charity (2 Peter 1:5,7).

Be of the same mind one toward another (Rom. 12:16).

It was raining. It had been raining as only in London it can rain, a steady downpour that interrupted the tour-group schedules.

Three groups sat in the lobby of the small hotel for two days. A German party occupied one corner of the lobby. They talked in their native tongue. A Japanese party of eight sat in another corner, conversing in their native tongue. The American contingent wandered restlessly about or sat in their corner of the lobby. The three groups communicated with each other in only small, vague ways. They asked each other simple questions such as, "Do you think it will ever stop raining? Too bad we're having to waste so much time sitting around. Does it always rain like this in London?"

It so happened that a mother and daughter were members of the American group, and that the eightieth birthday of the mother was coming up Friday.

The daughter, Anne, planned a special dinner in honor of the occasion. She conferred with the maitre d' and the chef, both of whom had tirelessly worked to make up for the weather's unruliness. They outdid themselves with special meat dishes and special desserts, belying the myth that food in England is atrocious.

The time for the birthday dinner arrived. Flowers appeared on the tables, but only on the tables of the American guests. After all, this was an American birthday party.

The dinner was magnificent: roast beef, Yorkshire pudding, salad in the best American tradition, soups. The chef prepared his famous English trifle: pound cake, well-drained apricots, whipped cream.

The Americans were seated in their accustomed corner, the Germans and Japanese on their own preserves. True, the others cast glances in the direction of the Americans. Enviously? Curiously? Who could say what was going on in their minds? When they spoke among themselves, they spoke in German or Japanese, of course.

Now came the climax of the affair. The maitre d', flanked by two white-jacketed waiters, entered the dining room. The maitre d' was bearing a huge birthday cake, complete with white frosting and pink candles.

The Americans rose as one in honor of the guest, Martha.

Once the cake was in place before her and she beamed her pleasure, the Americans began singing the "Happy Birthday" song. Martha wiped away happy tears.

Naturally, the Japanese and Germans had been watching this party. Suddenly, in the middle of the song, they began singing along with the Americans. What matter if they sang in their own tongue? Then, one by one, two by two, around the small dining room, the diners joined hands—Germans, Japanese, the few Britons. Hands reached out to the waiters and to the maitre d'. The circle was complete.

The song ended and a round of applause completed that part of the festivities. There were smiles and laughter.

The guests sat down. Martha turned her attention to the birthday cake. Solemnly, she closed her eyes for the traditional wish. She began cutting the cake.

Then another unexpected thing occurred. A tall German man in his fifties rose to face the guests. "May I say a word or two?" he asked, with a thick German accent. "Have you thought, my friends, and I mean all of you, we have been sitting here in this hotel for three days, and we have had no real communication until this occasion? For the first time we have really communicated through the universal language—music—and through our common day—the birthday anniversary. How much more we could have shown our common humanity if one of us had just taken the step to make it so. We share life, we share God, whom we worship, we share being in this hospitable country. I say, 'Thanks, God, for bringing us together at last.' I confess to a lump in my throat this minute. It proves to me I must reach out, touch others. My friends, we have wasted precious time. Let us not do so again. Let us always remember this international birthday party, a truly great experience."

Martha began cutting the cake as soon as the applause stopped. She cut it carefully, making the pieces small, so that everyone in the room might share in her special day.

Lord, we can be so close yet so far apart. We ask you to give us the sensitivity to reach out to others in our common humanity. We thank you for the little groups of people who have, through various events, touched each other in love. Increase our understanding of each other. We do give thanks for small but meaningful events in our lives. Amen.

11

Sunset? Sunrise?

If any man be in Christ, he is a new creature: old things are passed away; behold, all things are become new (2 Cor. 5:17).

Create in me a clean heart, O God; and renew a right spirit within me (Ps. 51:10).

I am the light of the world: he that followeth me shall not walk in darkness, but shall have the light of life (John 8:12).

For several years I had hanging over a chest in the living room a large picture a dear friend painted and gave to me. It is a land-and-seascape. Waves beat against the shore and two broken piers in the foreground. Rays of the sun streak through a slit in the cloudy sky. The colors in the painting are oranges, yellows, and dark browns.

Each night when I returned from work and entered the front door, I came face to face with that picture of a sunset. The day was finally finished. It was time to stop activity, and time for a certain sadness, too.

I sat in the chair opposite the picture and let the work of the day and the tiredness wash over me. I assessed my accomplishments and my failures. I admit I usually thought mostly of the failures. "Why did I do *that* today? Why was my coworker in such a surly mood? Why did I not accomplish more?" My glance invariably strayed to the sunset picture. My fears, frustrations, loneliness, a few resentments, and uncertainties seemed concentrated in that picture. It represented an unpeaceful ending to the day. Why did I not get rid of it? The answer is that I did like it. I treasured it because Vivian had given it to me as a remembrance when she moved up north.

Then I acquired another large picture, painted by another friend. The only place I could find for it was over the chest, facing the front door. But that brought on the problem of what to do with the sunset picture. The only place it fit was over the television, so I hung it there. It now faces the sofa as it hangs on the east wall of the living room.

But something suddenly happened to the sunset picture when I rehung it. It became a sunrise scene.

What did the sunrise mean to me when I began to contemplate it? It meant a new day had begun, a new day with its new set of challenges, a new day in which to anticipate joys, work, rest periods, and chatting with friends.

Now when I look at the picture I see less of the dark clouds, and the lonely broken pier. The browns serve to accent the bright oranges. The mood has changed from somber to cheerful, from representing a negative outlook and emotions to positive. The picture heralds a new day with new challenges. It promises a bright day!

Now while I sit on the sofa reading my daily morning

meditation or inspirational message, I have an added dimension—the sunrise picture.

I list my assets. I tend not to think so much of resentment as I do acceptance of others. When I look at myself I concentrate on my strengths, on my belief in a higher power. I anticipate myself rising to meet all problems with courage, and with kindness to other persons with whom I must deal. I feel a faith reborn. And as Tolstoy put it, "Faith is the force of life."

I have strength to meet this sunrise of a new day and to meet the day itself. I have not someone else's image of me, but my own self-image, and it is good, it is strong.

I may do foolish things—I probably will. But I will stop to collect my senses, rectify what I can, and turn away from the mistakes I cannot rectify.

I will walk tall and straight and strong today.

I look at Vivian's picture and I am doubly grateful for her friendship, and for the results of her talents that she shared with me.

Yes, the picture means a fresh start for each day, not the negatives that come with the tiredness after a busy day.

I have crossed another steppingstone of my life. The step I have just taken, I believe, has made me a better, stronger person, a more *human* human being. The life force of faith strengthens me.

Lord, thank you for the steppingstones of our lives, the steppingstones that lead us to development of our better selves, and to stronger faith. Thank you for our growth, and for your guidance. Thank you, for giving us the capacity to better understand the life you have given us each day. Amen.

12

Lights

Thy word is a lamp unto my feet, and a light unto my path (Ps. 119:105).

The light shineth in darkness; and the darkness comprehended it not (John 1:5).

God is light, and in him is no darkness at all (1 John 1:5).

Last night W dropped in just after dinner. He often does this. He had been mowing his lawn, and his clothes carried the fragrance of new-mown grass. How delightful is that peaceful look of someone who has been touching the earth and its growth.

"Let's take a ride into the mountains," he said.

We drove high, higher into our beloved nearby mountains. Elevations rose to 2000 feet, 4000 feet. At sharp turns we glanced back to see the lights of the three cities below. Red, yellow, green. Christmas in May!

We came to a small village. The summer season had not yet opened, so the streets were rolled up and put away for the night. Cafes and stores were dark except for feeble night lights. We did not linger. What was the use? No light.

We began the return, stopping frequently at turnoffs to feast on the sights below. View Point was our favorite because the many lights of the surrounding cities spread before us.

W asked, "Why do we enjoy lights so much?"

Yes, why? We talked about it.

When we were children, we thrilled to the lights of Christmas trees and decorations. Now we watch the flickering light of a candle and feel pleasure. We feel warm and comforted by lights shining in the windows of our homes when we return at night.

We welcome the light of a new day. How we welcome the sunlight after a siege of gloomy weather. How warm our skin feels when the light touches us.

We talked more about light. Why does a room light up when a certain type of person enters? Conversation stops; attention focuses on the person who is like a magnet drawing everyone's attention. Each person feels a touch of warmth.

We talked of the light in a baby's eyes when the mother enters the room, or when a bright toy (light, again) is dangled before the child.

We talked of the light in a lover's eyes, and of the light in our minister's face as he greets parishioners. We feel happiness when we see light in a loved one's or a friend's eyes.

And what does the Bible say of light? Memory served us well.

The Lord is my light and my salvation (Psa. 27:1).
The Lord shall be thine everlasting light (Isa. 60:20).
In him was life; and the life was the light of men (John 1:4).

I am the light of the world: he that followeth me shall not walk in darkness, but shall have the light of life (John 8:12).
Ye are the light of the world (Matt. 5:14).

W and I were silent then, observing the sea of lights below us. Our thoughts were deep, probing. Finally, W said, "I shall remember this experience. I know that my actions can be a light in the world. I can give love and understanding to people and be a light to them. I can be a light to myself by my own attitudes. Oh, there's so much I can do and give and be because of light!"

Lord, thank you for light. Thank you for the light of your love, your care. Thank you for the love of friends and family. Help us to always appreciate the warmth of light. We know it is of you and through you that we receive it. Amen.

13

Why?

We walk by faith, not by sight (2 Cor. 5:7).

Faith is the substance of things hoped for, the evidence of things not seen (Heb. 11:1).

Comfort yourselves together, and edify one another (1 Thess. 5:11).

This week has not been my week to try to simply manage my own problems and answer my own questions about life. It has been a week in which others put to me their personal questions. "Why, Mrs. Vandermey?"

Innocently enough I went to the television repair shop. All I wanted was a new tuning knob for my television set. I hoped I could simply buy it, return home, and replace the broken one, assuming my mechanical abilities were such that I could handle it. I had no hint anything of a philosophical nature was about to be presented to me.

I noticed Mrs. E, the shop owner's wife who works in the office, was limping. I did not ask why or what had happened since we last met. She might not want to talk about it.

But she did want to talk.

Thirty years had passed since the war during which she had lived in an Eastern European country. All that time she had carried pieces of shrapnel in her left knee and in her scalp, for she had been in the line of fire when her village was invaded.

The doctors she consulted after reaching this country advised leaving the pieces alone as long as they did not trouble her.

Four months ago, Mrs. E. and her husband realized a cherished dream, a visit to the Holy Land. On the fourth day of sightseeing, her knee began to pain. The joint gave out and she fell. She was hospitalized there, and again for surgery when she returned home. The surgery and post-surgery periods were traumatic. Medication caused her mind to reverberate, and she relived the terrors of her youth in the invaded village.

"Mrs. Vandermey," she cried as she finished telling her experience, "I'm scared. I relive those days. I shall not be able to walk again as I did before. Why? Am I being punished for visiting the holiest place on earth? Why?"

I shook my head. "I don't know," I replied helplessly. "I'm sorry. I wish I could give you an answer." Tears came to my eyes. Troubled by my own helplessness and troubled by Mrs. E's experience, I left.

Next day I visited a little boy of eight whom I helped with his schoolwork. A brain tumor had been discovered for which he was to have an operation. The parents were open in telling him he might not live.

He said to me, "Mrs. Vandermey, I'm scared. I prayed hard last night. I said, 'God, let's look at this situation. I have lots of things to do in my life. I'm planning to be a scientist. I'm going to try to find cures for lots of diseases. God, you'd better make me better in a hurry. I haven't got much time.' Why did this happen to me, Mrs. Vandermey?" The large brown eyes were tear-filled.

Not much time! Dear God, Timmy is only eight! "We have to pray, Timmy. We know God will help us through."

"I dunno," he replied.

At home I felt frustrated, weak, and ignorant. Why could I not answer these questions put to me the last two days? I could not even answer my own whys.

I called for an appointment with my minister. Surely he in his wisdom in dealing with many who surely also ask why could give me some answers.

My minister is a gentle person with an open and understanding heart. He leaned back in his huge office chair, rubbed a hand across his face, and asked, "What can I do for you today?"

I told him about Mrs. E and her question. I told him about Timmy and the brain tumor. I told him about my own frustration over my inability to answer the question, "Why must the righteous suffer?"

The pastor was silent for a long time. He sighed deeply. At last he spoke. "Theologians have pondered this question for ages, and the only place we can find the answer is in the Bible. Naturally, it's easy to know why the so-called sinners suffer." A twinkle came into his eyes. "They are apart from God. They do not love him."

"But why must Christians suffer? I've studied, I've tried to reason, I've listened to preachers," I said.

"Christians suffer so they may find communion with others who are suffering. They can be empathetic. The Bible also teaches that Christians suffer so they may glorify God in their lives. Remember the old saying, 'There are no atheists in foxholes.' In suffering we learn to rely on God and his will. He is the ultimate."

I said, "I've heard the Hopi Indians say God gave man free

will, a choice. Whatever you choose, you receive the consequences. But that doesn't take care of Mrs. E and Timmy."

My minister said, "Now we come to the matter of faith. We Christians need a growing faith. God is all, in all, through all, above all. We cannot know his mysteries while we live on this earth. And one of our hardest lessons to learn is that we do not have to understand or know the reasons for a circumstance. Our assignment is to trust God. Someday we will know. But for now, accept in faith."

Lord, give me faith. Amen.

14

The Do-nothing Day

Cast away from you all your transgressions; whereby ye have transgressed; and make you a new heart and a new spirit (Ezek. 18:31).

Whosoever drinketh of the water that I shall give him shall never thirst; but the water that I shall give him shall be in him a well of water springing up into everlasting life (John 4:14).

Now we have received, not the spirit of the world, but the spirit which is of God; that we might know the things that are freely given to us of God (1 Cor. 2:12).

I awakened, promising the day all sorts of accomplishments: housework, bills to be paid, phone calls, shopping. But suddenly, as often happens to many of us, the spirit was willing but the rest of me wasn't. Hands seemed chained; will to accomplish fled on the summer breeze. This day would surely turn into a do-nothing day. I tried, really tried, but still nothing happened. I confess to sinking momentarily into the pity pit, a sad place to be.

But a nudge came. A nudge from where? From way out there. Was it the Creator nudging me? Actually, the Creator had never been away. I had only thought the Creator to be at an unreachable distance. The nudge grew stronger.

I found myself awakening to creation. I began going about getting in touch with things.

I touched the carpet, running my hands across the soft pile. Oh, wool, where did you come from? I thought of sheep from whose wool the carpet had been made. I remembered seeing a lonely sheepherder on the hills of Spain watching his peaceful flock. But how could a man tending God's creatures be lonely? As I touched the pile of the carpeting, I began to feel the soft grazing land and see its luxuriant green.

Now I touched the wood of a favorite table. I have known it since childhood, for it belonged to my grandmother. As I ran my hand across the satin-smooth surface I thought of the forest from which the wood had been cut. Who had seen that the trees flourished? The Creator had, of course. He had provided the soil, the nutrients, the rain, the sun, and all things necessary for growth. He had given the lumbermen, the furniture maker, and the wood carver the knowledge to turn the wood into a lasting object of beauty. He had provided for our use.

I recalled a trip into the high Sierras, home of the giant redwoods. We stopped and walked over the crunchy needles. We paused and listened. The only sounds were of the wind rustling in the top branches. How soothing to city-bred ears! I sensed the sighing of the needles, reminding me of mysterious songs that stir and touch hearts with bitter sweetness.

So I spent the day touching things mentally as well as physically. No thought now of a wasted day. When there was no more indoors to touch, I went out-of-doors.

Now I experienced being touched. Yin and Yang, my neighbor's Siamese cats, came and rubbed against me. I petted them and they purred their feline songs in response.

Next, the perky Boston terrier from down the street, attached by a long leash to Mr. Bascomb, was taking Mr. Bascomb for a walk. Mr. Bascomb stopped, as usual, to brag about his boss, the dog. He complained as usual, about his hurting feet. I sympathized, as usual. The two went on around the block, and Mr. Bascomb was whistling.

Mrs. Trippet from across the street came out and called, "I've made cookies and fresh coffee. Come have some with me." Happily, I accepted.

We spent an hour exchanging news of families and friends and what was going on at church. Joe, her son, came in. He explained to me the details of how he was building a racing car. I pretended knowledge I did not possess; I do not know an alternator from a carburetor, but I felt obligated to do this pretending.

Suddenly, the day had slipped away. The sun melted into the hilltop to the west and sent out bright signals that said if we had any more tasks to complete before dark, we had best be about them.

I returned to the house, satisfied. I had accomplished much, not in the way of physical tasks, certainly, but much in mental satisfaction. I had a new appreciation of things and people and beauty. It had turned into a do-something-different day.

Lord, days of restlessness and aversion to tasks mean we need refreshment. You call us to stop for hours of appreciation of your world. You send your personal messages to us through the creatures, the forests, and our neighbors. You remind us you are with us in the forests, on the hilltops, in the valleys, with our neighbors, and in the streets. Thank you for the beauties and blessings of living. Amen.

15

The Kettle Huggers

For the work of a man shall he render unto him, and cause every man to find according to his ways (Job 34:11).

If any of you lack wisdom, let him ask of God (James 1:5).

Eyes have they, but they see not (Ps. 115:5).

They seeing see not; and hearing they hear not, neither do they understand (Matt. 13:13).

A wonderfully amusing story has come to us out of the legends of the Old West.

Some hunters went away from their camp for a short

while, but they left a kettle of water on the fire to heat it to the boiling point.

Along came an inquisitive bear. For a moment he watched the kettle lid bobbing up and down. But what intelligent bear could resist that bobbing lid? He seized the kettle.

What happened? Boiling water spilled out and scalded him. A bear's instinct is to hug more tightly that which hurts him, so the more tightly the bear hugged the kettle, the more he burned. The result was that the bear became completely disoriented.

I finished reading the story and was at the same time sympathizing with and laughing at the bear's situation, when Jane, my neighbor came. I told her the story.

Together we laughed, and then she grew pensive. Jane always looks beneath the surface. She said, "I wonder what happens to us humans when we hug something too tightly."

We let our minds wander and suppose. The first example we thought of was the mother who will not, or cannot, let go of her children. As they struggle for independence, which is their right and is perfectly normal, the mother hugs them more tightly, but with words rather than physical hugs. "Look what I've done for you. How can you do this to your mother? How can you leave me in my old age? You don't love me, or you wouldn't . . ."

What happens? More often than not, the child breaks away, leaving a lonely saddened mother who can only pray for her child's safety or for God to somehow bring him back. And often God's answer is, "No." A real kettle hugger, this mother, because she hurts so very much.

Jane thought of another kettle hugger, the wife who must know where her husband is every minute. He must account for his every move. Is he able to do this for long? When will resentment begin to set it? "Soon," Jane said.

Another kettle hugger, too young to understand, is the child who hugs his new toy too closely so no one else can touch it. The toy is crushed. Brokenhearted, the child cries.

For an hour Jane and I listed kettle huggers, such as the

business tycoon, or the athlete who is an overachiever. Laughing, we also included ourselves among the kettle huggers.

What can we call ourselves when we nurse our aches and pains and slights and imagined snubs, and refuse to let them go? Laughing, Jane said, "Ailment huggers."

But what of remedies?

We posed solutions. The mother, even though she is hurting when her child attempts to break away, can say, "I love you. I pray for you. Any time you need me, I'm here." The child hugging his toy to the breaking point can learn to share.

Jane summed it up, "We all learn—we hope—to let go of a treasure and know something good is still in store for us.

"We turn our aches and pains and frustrations over to the great healer, who hears us when we pray. Just thinking about God takes our minds off the hurts, the frustrations, the disappointments. Know God is love. He must love us; otherwise, why are we here? In giving our kettles to God we set ourselves free."

Lord, often we are selfish, wanting our own ways. Or we want certain people who are dear to us to stay closer to us than is good for them. Teach us your way, Lord. We know your love and help are free for the asking. But you leave us free to choose what we will do with them. Direct us to turning our lives and those of our loved ones over to you and so find our ultimate security. Amen.

16

Push that Button Again

The desire accomplished is sweet to the soul (Prov. 13:19).

Which of you, intending to build a tower, sitteth not down first, and counteth the cost, whether he have sufficient to finish it? (Luke 14:28).

I have not run in vain, neither laboured in vain (Phil. 2:16).

Let us go on unto perfection (Heb. 6:1).

Are you set in your ways? Join the crowd. Our set ways are comfortable, but at times they can be boring, perhaps even loathsome, to us. How can we change, without too much pain, the patterns we have lived in so long?

We try to resign ourselves to being somewhat habit bound, continuing to prefer the same types of food, or wearing more or less the same style of clothing because we think it best suits us. Still, we are not quite satisfied with this sameness.

I was unhappy with my own continuing state of sameness and my inability to change until I made a discovery one day.

At a downtown intersection, the traffic was heavy. A little lady carrying a cane was pushing the walk button of the signal light. She pushed and pushed and pushed.

"Doesn't she know," I thought, "that it doesn't make any difference? The pattern of the signal is set. It turns the light green for so long and it turns the light red for so long. We can't do anything about it." Impulsively, I asked the woman, "Why do you keep pushing the button over and over?"

The little lady gave me a how-dare-you look and replied, "If you keep pushing the button over and over, the waiting time gets shorter. That's because there's a mechanism that counts the number of pushes. It then knows how many people are waiting to cross the street and lets me go. I change the pattern by pushing the button over and over."

Was this true? How was I to know? I know nothing about computers, except that they get me into trouble occasionally. The light turned green for the little lady with the cane, and triumphantly she crossed the street.

I began to think about my habit-changing problem. One push of a button doesn't change my life. Well, how about pushing again and again to change the pattern?

At home I examined a picture I had been painting without achieving the results I wanted. I looked at it from this angle and that, pushing mental buttons. There! The perspective had been wrong. Now I was satisfied. I had pushed the button one more time.

I began to think of our great inventors, such as Edison. Certainly, this brilliant man, during the night hours he worked in his laboratory, pushed thousands of mental buttons before he finally achieved success.

"What happens when we push the mental buttons repeatedly?" I mused. It may be that our mental mechanisms, our sensors, our intuitions, grow tired of the constant stimulation and finally give in. Perhaps the mind finally says, "Well, if you want a different answer, if you insist on it, I'll give it to you. I'm tired of resisting!"

So I learned from the little lady pushing the button repeatedly that if I push my mental buttons often enough, I'll be able to change a habit and start a fresh pattern. Who knows, I may want to change it, too, sometime.

Lord, thank you for the gift of being able to learn. At every chance meeting with another person I may learn something new. Grant that my mind will remain flexible and my fingers nimble enough to push buttons often enough to obtain the desires and satisfy the needs of my life. I know you will lead me to push the right buttons, and for that I am grateful. Amen.

17

The Negatives and the Positives

I would have you wise unto that which is good, and simple concerning evil (Rom. 16:19).

Whatsoever things are true, whatsoever things are honest, whatsoever things are just . . . whatsoever things are lovely, whatsoever things are of good report; if there be any virtue, and if there be any praise, think on these things (Phil. 4:8).

When I was in the downtown area I stopped to look at the blackened ruins of two businesses. It had been a three-alarm fire, vicious and destructive. Twisted metal beams lay sprawled about as if some angry giant had turned on them. The roof had buckled and lay on top of other debris. Washing machines, dryers, and refrigerators were the hopeless victims.

Fire can be destructive or constructive.

In contrast to the ruinous fire, I think about fire's benefits to me, such as for heat with which to prepare food and to heat water for bathing. I sit before a fire with friends, contentedly warmed in heart as well as body. I dream dreams watching the flickering flames.

My thinking leads to other things that can be both negative and positive.

Love: selfish or generous.

I think of an acquaintance. She loves her husband and her children, who are married and have their own families. But this woman loves her family so much she wants (unconsciously, I'm certain) to go to their graves with them. "You ought to be more saving," she tells her daughter, who has just made the important purchase of a new washer and dryer. To her husband she says, "You could save the money you spent on that new car; the other one was good enough. I don't know why the children don't come more often. After all, we are their parents." So the family struggles between guilt and nonguilt. Strangling love can be as destructive as a three-alarm fire.

On the other hand, a wise and truly loving parent I knew who said to a daughter about to leave to seek a career in New York, "This is not what I wanted for you. But if this is what you truly want, you have my blessing and my prayers. I chose my life's work. I will not deny you the same privilege. I love you too much."

Food: Excessive or basic.

Stand before a smorgasbord or a potluck. We want to sample everything, it all looks so good. But it's stuffed with calories—fats, sugar. Lord, deliver me from potlucks! Inevitably, I overindulge. I feel miserable. I will gain weight. I may even be ill.

But, of course, we need food. It nourishes our bodies. Our

bodies grow and thrive on it. Without food, what would we be?

My words: discouraging or encouraging.

Suppose I criticize my friends because they do not act the way I believe they should? Do I not become an ego shatterer? Am I not liable to crush a dream, an ambition?

A famous minister put it this way. "If I have an impulse to criticize someone for a behavior of which I do not approve (and believe me, I have many such impulses), I caution myself to silence. Is that person not acting out of his own level of understanding, out of his mental and cultural development? If it is a friend I have my critical eye on, I must remember that he was my friend before I knew of his idiosyncrasies. Is he any less my friend now? Of course not, and I will stand by him the way he is."

If a destructive word does escape our lips, what then? "I'm sorry" are two short words, but they can make or break friendships. The unsaid "I'm sorry" leaves us being less than we believe ourselves to be.

Attitudes: destructive or constructive.

I see a rattletrap car on the street ahead. I am tempted to think, Why doesn't that man take better care of his car? But I am humbled into a different attitude when I consider that catastrophe may have struck the family. Perhaps the man is out of work and is struggling to hold his life together. Immediately my thoughts change to sympathy and understanding.

And I must deal with my attitudes toward myself. I am guilt ridden when I leave some important task undone. Oh! My errors! Mountainous guilt! I will not let the errors be. But, if I do not live up to my expectations of myself, if I make errors, or if I leave tasks undone, I can try to forgive myself, knowing I am human and, therefore, fallible. Humbly, I can pray, "Lord, forgive me. I'm trying!" And my effort becomes success.

Lord, we live in all kinds of situations with all kinds of people. Living with ourselves is often hardest of all. Help us to see the good side of things, to utilize the positives for constructive ends. Give us the power to remedy potentially bad situations, so that the world may be a better place because we have passed this way. Amen.

18

Grandmother's Personal Progress Report

The righteous also shall hold on his way, and he that hath clean hands shall be stronger and stronger (Job 17:9).

A wise man will hear, and will increase learning (Prov. 1:5).

When that which is perfect is come, then that which is in part shall be done away (1 Cor. 13:10).

If we love one another, God dwelleth in us, and his love is perfected in us (1 John 4:12).

When I was a child, I often stopped on the way home from school to visit my grandmother. She would regularly give me her personal progress report. Was it her way of trying to teach me how to live?

Recently, in going through some of her papers I inherited, I discovered her own account of her efforts to become a better person, her efforts to grow and to dare. The pages were yellowed, the ink faded, but the message written in her precise hand was clear.

"Please, Diary, don't think I'm patting myself on the back, that I'm being egotistical. But it pleases me to tell myself, 'Nora, you're improving. One day you'll be able to call yourself a first-class Christian.'

"Once, I had a habit of listing my frustrations, my problems, and who did what to me. Just like a grocery list.

"Now, after some mighty struggling I still have the frustrations and problems, but I try to reason with myself. Don't mistake me, I'm wise enough to know I'll always have problems: having them is a sign I'm alive. The moment I no longer have them, I'll no longer be on this earth.

"After a savage battle with myself, I became convinced breaking the treasured pitcher was not a major catastrophe, though I know I'll regret its loss. I know too, if someone steps on my tender mental toes, I am able to think, 'That's the way she is. What I said to her in the first place was not what I really meant to say. Why couldn't she understand? But she did not. I forgive myself for such clumsy speech. I forgive her for misunderstanding me.' This is rather complicated. But then, I'm rather complicated."

Another day Grandmother wrote, "Now when I have a dull day, rather than fret, I tell myself 'Better relax your body and mind, because you know very well your life is never dull for long. Your mind needs a rest period, just as there must be rests in musical compositions to make the music more interesting.'

"As I said, it is a savage battle to become an adult. Few of us have the enlightenment, the strength, the courage to do it. But I know I must do this battle or I'll go downhill like a sled on a steep slope."

The entry of another day says, "My neighbors may wonder why I get in my car and go out into the country by way of the freeway. I admit to apprehension (I almost wrote fear!). But I know I must forever abandon the search for security and take the risk of not knowing outcomes. I will learn a little each day to have faith in God. Only in this way will I learn. I must fling my arms open and embrace life—whatever it presents. As Robert Frost said, 'Life is a risk and I took it.'"

As I read my grandmother's diary, I thought her to be almost melodramatic; yet, I remembered that was the way she was: high spirited, covering her worries with a laugh, or at least a smile.

She wrote on. "Doubt, darkness, even fear are parts of life. So I am stubbornly optimistic in times of uncertainty, knowing the Lord will carry me through.

"So I live today and tomorrow as they come. I learn as time passes most of my worries are self-made. My imagination is the hyper kind. I've become quite familiar with this over the years. I know it can be my worst enemy. Yet, knowing this is half the battle.

"So I say to myself, 'See, you were only imagining things. Like a child. Nothing bad happened. Your friends did not or had not left you as you thought. Neither have your friends rejected you. Your friends, too, have problems. And so does your family.'

"I know this, too: God has helped me by putting this urge in me to improve myself so that I will be better deserving of His bounty. It may even be my way of saying thanks for life's blessings."

Lord, thank you for grandparents who give us guidance. We learn from them that we are not born with ready-made wisdom. We are not born adult. We are born babies. As we grow, we progress and we learn. We do not become complete. Try as we do, we know we do not achieve the perfection we so earnestly seek. But we know, from our constant communion with you, you give us strength. For all this we do give thanks. Amen.

19

What's Wrong with a Happy Day?

He that is of a merry heart hath a continual feast (Prov. 15:15).

The joy of the Lord is your strength (Neh. 8:10).

God giveth to a man that is good in his sight wisdom, and knowledge, and joy (Eccles. 2:26).

The checker bagged the customer's groceries and handed the package to her. "Thanks for shopping with us. Have a happy day!"

The customer scowled, grabbed her package, and said, "You don't care if I have a happy day. You don't care any more than as if I were your enemy. You only want to make money off me!" She marched away, head held high.

Several customers in line smiled pityingly. Tears came to the checker's eyes. But she brushed them aside and, smiling, turned to the next person in line.

Someone remarked, "Poor dear, she doesn't know what a good day is. I'd like to stuff her with happiness."

A philosopher once said, in effect, "Whatever irritates us, or makes us feel uncomfortable, is merely a reflection of our own thoughts. Shall we blame someone else, or ourselves? It's easier to blame the other person. But let's look first at our own thoughts."

I began to wonder. Do we blame the other person when we are made uncomfortable by a chance remark, however pleasant the remark? What is going on inside us when we react negatively to another person's remark or action?

I decided to do an experiment. No matter how I felt, happy or not-so-happy, I would always speak to people cheerfully or sympathetically when I was out shopping.

One day a checker looked tired and harrassed. I remarked, "I believe you've had a hard day."

A warm smile came to her face. "It must be one of those days when I can't do anything right. Thanks for helping me get through the day!"

"I know how you feel. Some of my days aren't all sunshine either." That brought a giant smile.

So the days went. At the mall, at the post office, and whether or not I felt like it, I said, "Have a good day."

I thanked the waitress for good service at lunch. So what if the salad was slightly wilted, and the coffee not to my liking? The waitress had not prepared it.

Later, in a note to the management of the cafe, I made polite suggestions for improvements. The management was truly grateful, grateful to the extent of sending me a voucher for two free dinners at the cafe. Well, now I was the happy person, paid for being cheerfully helpful!

For two weeks I continued the experiment. Most people

returned my good wishes. Only occasionally would someone reply, "What's so good about today?"

I resisted the temptation to give an argument to that question—that he was alive, that the sun was shining , that it would rise tomorrow at the proper time, that. . . . Well, I could have gone on and on, but he wouldn't have listened. He was hurting inside and tried to take out the hurt on me.

During this time, I did not have the attitude of being Little Miss Sunshine. I was coolly experimenting.

When the two weeks were over, I did my tabulating. Can you believe, the positive responses were far, far ahead of the negatives?

But that isn't the sum of it. I felt happy. Many of my personal problems seemed to have diminished or disappeared completely, and I was better able to cope with the remaining problems.

I also reached some personal conclusions. Emotional balance is certainly tied to our reactions to what happens to us, to our attitudes, which are either positive or negative. But it's up to us to choose how we will react and tailor our attitudes.

I shall not soon forget the lesson I learned trying to make happier days. And, after all, what's wrong with happy days?

Lord, often we don't feel like smiling; often we do not even want others to try to give us happy days. Help us each day to keep at the front of our minds, our knowledge of our abilities to cope, and help us to cope cheerfully. Make us aware of your being with us each day so that we are one with you. Amen.

20

Selves

Behold, I go forward (Job 23:8).

Be ye therefore perfect, even as your Father which is in heaven is perfect (Matt. 5:48).

I have planted, Apollos watered; but God gave the increase (1 Cor. 3:6).

The wives living on Laurel Court met once a month for coffee. They named their club the Self Club. Each month members reported on the selves they had been concentrating on, the discoveries they had made about themselves, and how many selves they found they possessed.

Of course, there was much laughter as well as much seriousness in the conversation. And a number-one rule was that there were to be no contradictions after members had discussed their discoveries.

They kept a journal to read back at times so they could check themselves.

Toni talked on being *self-sufficient:*

"That means I can handle affairs. I do not lean on someone else, except in times of distress or real need. I try to be aware of my inner strength as well as my outer strength. I try to solve problems myself. I love myself too much to be a leaner."

Jean on *self-improvement:*

"By constant work, by love of ourselves and therefore of the Creator who made our lives possible, we constantly look for ways of improving our minds and our attitudes. We try to be kind and understanding. We work to keep our minds and bodies healthy and strong."

Beth on *self-determination:*

"My life from day to day is in many ways determined by the self within. What kind of self do I possess? I look in the mirror and I see the image of myself, but I also see deeper than that. I see the God in me. God is love. Do I run out of this love? I know if I am angry, discouraged, and want to give up I am not being loyal to the God within me. I can choose to be negative or positive. I have self-determination."

Jean on *self-control:*

"I'm glad I have developed self-control. Well, most of the time." She laughed at herself. "I'd really lose my mind if I didn't have self-control. Two teenagers flying in and out of the house wanting to be taken to football practice or to parties. A husband, efficient in business but careless about the car, even about the clothes he wears. But I relax and tell myself I love them, so I'd better love them the way they are." Her eyes were bright with happiness, her face serene.

Martha on *self-discovery:*

"Matthew 7:7 puts it this way: 'Ask, and it shall be given you; seek, and ye shall find; knock, and it shall be opened to you.' Well! I look. I discover the universe is filled with God, and I know He is as close to me as my breath. I am part of this wonderful whole. I am ecstatic. I belong. I see the world now through love; therefore, I see beauty. I have a place in it all. Now my self is greater than I ever dreamed."

Georgia on what is *self-evident:*

"I thought a lot about this and about the old saying, 'I can't see the forest for the trees.' What does this mean to me? I am so involved with the details of a project, I gnaw at them, worrying and fretting so much that I forget the whole of the project. Eventually I remember: Take one thing at a time. It is self-evident that you can't make a cake by just stirring the ingredients in the bowl with a spoon. There are further steps to take to make the whole cake. Easy does it. I relax. All is well."

Ann on being *self-contained:*

"I think of how this differs from self-control. The birth of a baby, the birth of a puppy or a kitten are miracles of God's work. Each baby, each puppy or kitten is complete, perfect. And miracle of miracles, at any time in our lives when things have gone wrong, either because of our own selves or by the mistakes of another, we can begin again like infants. We can rebuild. We each have the potential for growth to completion of God's will for us, while the strength of God is still with us."

Faye on *self-examination:*

"This is not easy. Too often I examine myself and my life and I do not like what I find under my mental microscope. I want to be whole, complete, perfect, but I am not. I do not want to be critical of others, yet somehow I want them to act according to my ideas. That isn't right. I go through periods of discouragement because I feel I've failed to be the person I want to be. Then I remember I am part of the great mystery of life. I have strength of mind and spirit and body. That's what happens when we self-examine in a positive way. I am worth salvaging." Faye smiled.

The group continues with other selves: self-esteem, self-help, self-confidence, self-improvement, self-reliance. Each member adds to the list and takes away with her something of the growth of the other members.

Lord, as the poet said, "My ship is so frail, and the seas are so stormy," so we all need your strength. We seek the shelter of your love in working to make our selves more and more each day of what you want and expect them to be. Amen.

21

A Day for God to Laugh

Go thy way, eat thy bread with joy, and drink thy wine with a merry heart (Eccles. 9:7).

Ointment and perfume rejoice the heart: so doth the sweetness of a man's friend by hearty counsel (Prov. 27:9).

For more years than the members care to remember, the foursome has been meeting one Saturday each month for lunch. Oh, there have been lapses—time out for vacations, for family problems—but as regularly as they can, they meet. The lunches are simple. The talk also is simple (meaning idiotic, they say), pure girl-talk. Husbands' banishment for the day permits that.

At first the conversation is serious. What to do about this

child or that. How to deal with husband problems and self-problems. What colors to use in redecorating. And isn't the price of meat out of sight!

But over the years the talk has changed. The moods have changed. Widowhood has come to two. Illness fills the life of another. Ailments, temporary or permanent, have come. Three have moved to different houses.

The four are still busy. One has a daily job. The widows have a succession of men friends. The others have problems. They have accepted change as part of living.

Dottie is in the throes of a new romance. But she will somehow escape. She has lived alone too long to deal with the problems of a new marriage, in spite of her regard for the man. But for now the male company is a nice change.

Marge must now use a cane, which she laughs about. It makes a fine weapon—just in case.

Radie has a boss who would do well to find a menial job.

Yes, they know each other well. But, unfortunately, they do not read minds. They do not remember dates, either, not necessarily because of memory lapses, but because of busyness.

Jean prepared lunch one Saturday, but the guests did not arrive. Why? Jean had the right hour, but the wrong Saturday. Even after three years, she still threatens to serve the by-now-green chicken salad she prepared that day.

Once, one member forgot she had a luncheon date at Jean's. The resulting telephone call brought her rushing in haphazardly dressed for the party. More laughter about failing minds.

The laughter continues over the rolls that burned because the hostess was listening to the chatter in the living room. More laughter over the latest man friend to go helps to stop the tears of the sad member.

When the four are seated at the table, Jean says grace. Jean says it best, so the others say, because she is Catholic. For years the tone of the prayers was serious, with thanks to God for the food, for the loving hands which prepared it, and for friendships enduring over the years.

But now, the four say, how God must laugh. They decide it is his day, and doesn't he deserve a laugh now and then? Doesn't it cause him to relax to sit back and listen in on his silly children?

So Jean says in her prayer, "God, here are your silly children again. We are all together at last. Lord, Radie did think it was her turn to prepare lunch when it was really Dottie's turn. We ask you to forgive Marge for burning the rolls. We do not need rolls anyway, Lord. At least two of us could lose a few pounds."

A pause for laughter.

"Lord, please don't let Dottie lose her head and do anything foolish, like getting married. Please protect her, for she is a child."

Again a pause for laughter.

"Lord, we will not say anything wise today. We will simply be foolish and silly. We will not have time for gossip and grumbles about the weather, about the neighbors, or about aches and pains."

More laughter and a return to composure.

"We are grateful Dottie did not forget the day for our lunch. We are grateful to you, Lord, for being the glue which has held us together for so long. We are grateful we are able to laugh at our wrinkles and sagging muscles, and that we have sense enough not to eat food our digestive systems can no longer tolerate.

"We thank you for this food. We are thankful for each other. We even thank you for the trials you have given us. Working through our problems strengthens us. Our abilities to get here under our own power proves you have given us strength, plus some mental capabilities, despite our years. Amen."

The lighthearted luncheon begins. The girl-talk continues. The afternoon is filled with laughter and chatter. Complete relaxation radiates from the four.

The date for the next meeting is set, provided, of course, a daughter does not send out an SOS, a man friend does not interfere, a husband does not require attention—so many provideds. Nonetheless, there will be another luncheon.

Lord, we thank you for enduring friendships. We thank you we can come to you with laughter. We thank you for understanding us with all the vagaries of human nature you have given us. We know you must sometimes wonder how it is possible you could have created such as ourselves. But we relax in the knowledge you are our indulgent Father and do understand us. Amen.

22

What Is Bread?

Bear ye one another's burdens, and so fulfill the law of Christ (Gal. 6:2).

The stranger that dwelleth with you shall be unto you as one born among you, and thou shalt love him as thyself (Lev. 19:34).

The refugee, a small, dark-bearded man from an oppressed country, had sought and found asylum in the United States and been accepted into its society. Sponsored by the members of a church congregation, he was now well-settled, having a good job and proudly sustaining himself.

One Sunday he requested permission to say a few words before the minister's sermon.

Hands clasped, he stood at the pulpit. He said, "We have

just said the Lord's Prayer. I wonder exactly what it means to you. The time will be too long to tell you what all the parts of it means to me. I want to take just one word: bread.

"Not long ago, before I escaped to this country, I was in a jungle. I did not know where I was. I had no shelter. When I came here you gave me shelter. That, to me, is bread.

"I had no clothes on my back for I had no shirt. Now I have a shirt. That, to me, is bread.

"I was scared the enemy would come and find me as they had my family. They did not find me, and after months of being on the water and being shot at and having no food, I was allowed to come to this country. Life. That is bread. Though I mourn for my family, I have a new family. You. That is bread.

"When I came here I had no money. I could not speak your language. You helped me. I learned the language—well, pretty good. I have a job. I can keep myself. That, to me, is bread. I have money in my pockets to buy what I need. Bread, bread.

"I stand here. I can say what I think. I can say my beliefs in God. I have no fear of being put in a dungeon for what I say, or shot, or tortured. Bread.

"I walk down the streets of this town and people speak to me as if I were someone. I am no longer at the bottom of the heap, as you say. Bread. My daily bread has come to me.

"If I ache from tiredness at my job, my boss at the plant asks if I am not feeling well. And sometimes I am not. I was without food for a long time, and my body is not yet strong. My boss says, how do you put it?, 'Take it easy awhile.' Bread.

"I hated my government, and lots of people, for a long time for what it has done to my family and me. Now, I no longer hate. Hate is poison. Now, I silently bless because through you and your goodness to me, I can no longer hate. Bread for my heart.

"Mornings, I waken to the shining sun, the sky, the nice houses and the businesses. My soul rises to meet the sun; it is a day when I will have work and time for play, too. Bread.

"I needed love and care when I came here. My soul seemed dead. How long had it been since a person had said a nice word to me? I cannot remember. Now I go along the streets. I have only kind words spoken to me. Do you know what that means to me? Bread. I can and do love again. Once I was sure my heart was dead, though it kept me breathing. Bread.

"Sharing. I have friends to my place. We laugh. I cook one of my native dishes. And there is brotherhood. Love of man for man. Bread. I receive much bread. I give back what bread I can. Someday I will give more. That, too, is bread, for it feeds my heart."

With palms together, the speaker bowed to the audience. "I thank you for hearing me." Still bowing, he turned to the minister. "Thank you for letting me speak."

The congregation rose as a unit. Heads automatically bowed, hands joined spontaneously.

Someone began to speak softly, with deep feeling. "Our Father who art in heaven, hallowed be thy name." Never had the people said the prayer with such deep sincerity.

The prayer ended, the congregation was seated. The minister stood at the lectern. He, too, spoke softly. "I do not feel capable of delivering the sermon I had prepared for you today; you have already had an inspiring lesson this day. We will have an hour of fellowship instead. I, for one, have experienced a revelation. The Lord's Prayer will forever have special meaning for me, and I am sure for us all. My friend, thank you. You have given us bread."

Lord, we thank you for this new appreciation of life about us, for the many blessings we so often let pass unnoticed. Open our eyes to life's applications of your word. Make us always be mindful of what you would have us do. Amen.

23

I Remember Them Well

Whatsoever thy hand findeth to do, do it with thy might (Eccles. 9:10).

Feed my lambs (John 21:15).

Let every one of us please his neighbor for his good to edification (Rom. 15:2).

The afternoon program for the church women's club was unusual. Each member was to think of some person whom she remembered well for a kind word or deed.

One member laughingly protested, "That's hard to do. It seems I always remember the people it's hard to remember fondly."

"I know what you mean," another member responded.

Nevertheless, the group set to work. Except for a few sighs and comments like, "Oh, this is hard," the soft sounds of pens against slips of paper filled the room.

Later, each member read her I-remember-them-well comment.

Jean told this story, "I was on a lonely gravel detour road. The car bounced hard, and even though I drove slowly, the engine just plain died.

"I got out of the car and looked around. There were no houses nearer than a half mile. I started out to get help. I'd walked awhile when I heard a car coming behind me. I was scared. This was no place for a woman alone. The car came up beside me. A bearded young man with two small children beside him was in the car. 'Something wrong?' he asked. When I told him, he replied, 'Perhaps I can fix it.'

"The sight of that kind face and those two dear children quieted my fears of being alone and in trouble. The man spent a half-hour repairing my car. Some wires had jiggled loose. I offered him money, but he refused. 'We're on this earth to help others,' he said. Neither would he let me give his children a little money. 'They must learn, too.'

"I remember him well."

Margot spoke next. "I remember well my eighth-grade teacher. I had been ill most of the semester and was way behind in math. She remained after school to tutor me and refused to take any money for her work. I then took the exams and passed. I remember her well."

Jennie said, "I remember the homemade soups my mother made for me after she came home from a long, hard day's work at the shop she operated. She was desperately tired, but she knew I loved her soups and she loved me. She worked hard to save money for my college tuition."

Another member read, "I always thought my neighbor was involved only with himself, that he was selfish. But one day, I was trying in my clumsy way to roll up the garden hose after washing the car. He came over and said, 'Let me show you how.' Patiently, he laid one end down and then slowly, in a relaxed way, began coiling it. He hung it up for me. Now every time I hang up that hose, nicely coiled because of his kindness in showing me, I remember him well."

Faith said, "I remember so well a little boy. He must have been ten years old. He offered to carry my heavy grocery bags to the car for me, and gladly I let him. As he walked away after I'd thanked him, I noticed he had only one arm and wore a brace on his left leg. It flashed through my mind he may have been one of the thalidomide children. He lived to help others." Faith wiped away a tear. "He was making himself so worthwhile despite his handicap."

There were many more I-remember-them-wells. After all the members had read their contributions, Phyllis added, "This reminds me too late to put on paper, but I remember so well my minister's constant help and prayers when I was going through a bad time in my life. He was at my side constantly, a true servant of God. I remember, too, the troubled teenager who often came to our house and poured out his troubles. Before he finally left town to go live with a relative, he first made a special trip to see us. He said, 'I'll always remember you and how you listened to me and never condemned me. You heard me with love.' My husband cried, and I did, too."

Margaret commented, "This has been a real building experience for me. It makes me think, 'How do I want to be remembered? For a kindness? For an unkindness?' I know what the answer is. I know, too, that, unconsciously, as I think of someone, I remember that someone by connecting the person with the deed."

Jean ended the session. She spoke directly to the program chairwoman. "Martha, what an experience, what an inspiration we've all had today as you asked us to remember people's good deeds. I'm sure you've helped us change our thinking, not only about others, but about ourselves in more ways than one. We will remember you well."

Lord, thank you for our experiences with other people

from which we benefit and which lead us to new and enriching endeavors. With your constant help in the richness of your love, we can in turn brighten another's life. May we ourselves be remembered well. Amen.

24

Times My Father Took Off for Chicago

If a man think himself to be something, when he is nothing, he deceiveth himself (Gal. 6:3).

If I justify myself, mine own mouth shall condemn me (Job 9:20).

Every way of a man is right in his own eyes: but the Lord pondereth the hearts (Prov. 21:2).

When my mother cleaned house she really meant it. The cleaning woman arrived early. Draperies and curtains came down, furniture was piled onto porches, scatter rugs came up and the carpet cleaners rushed in. The vacuum cleaner hummed and the washer chugged itself into exhaustion. Bedding hung on the lines, flapping in spring or fall winds. Dishes were hauled from cupboards, washed, and placed on freshly lined shelves.

This upheaval lasted a week, twice a year.

What happened to the family during these times? While my mother insisted that God insisted on clean houses, and that a good mother properly cared for her family by having a clean house, the family didn't exactly agree with my mother and God.

The children played outside as much as possible, or went to the neighbors' homes where life was normal.

My father, sensing the onset of these semiyearly upheavals, and rejecting my mother's words about the will of God, packed his bags and took off for Chicago. "Where a man can have some peace and quiet," was the way he put it.

As the years passed and the semiyearly cleanings came on schedule, the trips to Chicago lasted longer and longer. And with every cleaning season my mother became increasingly unhappy, because the family was unhappy. "I want to be a good Christian," she said, and was caught between her sense of duty to cleanliness and her desire for her family's happiness.

One recent evening my friend Anne came in while I was remembering these incidents from my childhood. She sat down in her favorite chair, the chair she sits in when she wants to confess something she has done displeasing to herself.

Without preliminaries, she said, "My, I was good today! I offered to take my neighbor to the doctor. I did it by sacrificing club meeting. I baked a cake for the church dinner. It was lavish with chocolate and nuts. I was proud of that cake, just as I was proud I'd sacrificed to take my neighbor to the doctor. They were such Christian things to do. I felt so sanctimonious because I could overlook the fact she likes to impose on people. Oh, I wanted to please the Lord! All day I was determined to please him. I surely wanted him to see what a good Christian I am.

"I was good in other ways, too. I thought only good thoughts about everyone. Not once did I ask what the world is coming to, though I admit I did wonder.

"Still, I was not good because I *wanted* to be. I was determined to be a good Christian, whether I liked it or not." She paused for breath. "But do you know, I'm not the least bit happy tonight? I did not do those things because I wanted to. I did them out of duty and to curry God's favor. I did good works with my mind but not my heart."

Anne and I talked about it. One of us remembered Ecclesiastes 7:16: "Be not righteous over much; neither make thyself over wise; why should thou destroy thyself?" Then there is Galatians 5:22, 23: "The fruit of the spirit is . . . temperance." We recalled the Pharisees, who were vainglorious in their good works.

We decided to do less of what we were doing that merely looked good on us. Rather, we knew that what we do with the heart and do wholeheartedly is what is pleasing to God and to ourselves, and results in the genuine kindness appreciated by others.

Anne concluded the discussion. "Your mother and I are prime examples of what we're discussing. No wonder your father took off for Chicago. Yes, it's better to act out of heartfelt love than to serve up what passes for love just to make ourselves look good."

Lord, remind us to always leaven our cakes and breads—deeds of kindness—with love. We know that good deeds done out of mere duty really build walls between ourselves and our friends and families, and ultimately between ourselves and you. We thank you for opening our minds to your truths. Amen.

25

Boy's Eye-view of His Country

Out of the mouth of babes and sucklings thou hast perfected praise (Matt. 21:16).

In the lips of him that hath understanding wisdom is found (Prov. 10:13).

The fifth-grade teacher proudly showed me a report one of her students, Randall, had written after a field trip to the city's and county's government headquarters. "It's seldom a teacher learns whether or not her students have ever really learned anything on these trips," she said. "Through this report I learned to appreciate all Randall saw, and I am thankful to God for all the blessings he has given me in our country. The report gave me a new slant."

Here is what Randall wrote. "Yesterday our fifth-grade class went to visit our city hall and county courthouse. I saw many things I never saw before. I was proud of the buildings. I thanked God I live here. We walked along the outside of the city hall first. I thought, Why, this belongs to me. My dad pays taxes to keep this going. Look at the flowers, look at the pretty lawn and the trees so heavy with green leaves. And there are the gardeners keeping it all trimmed and green. It was the same at the county courthouse where the men of the law see that laws are obeyed and bad people learn it doesn't pay to be bad and not obey the laws.

"I looked at the marble, I looked at the paintings on the wall. I thought, We own this, too. It is ours. I am proud. I am proud I can say this. Lots of people in this world cannot say that about their government houses.

"I wish I had known all this when my father and mother took me to Washington, D.C. last year. I saw the beautiful buildings. I saw the statue of Lincoln with the beautiful pool in front of it. I saw the White House and the Capitol. I saw the cathedral where people go to worship God. I saw the beautiful flowers and the grass. I did not think then that this belongs to me, to all of us. But I do now and I am proud.

"Now every time I go downtown I think about these things. I pass the firehouse where all the men are waiting to answer a call to some emergency, like a fire or if somebody is having a heart attack. The paramedics will race to the fire with the firemen and they will put out the fire and help people who are hurt. I talked with my father about this and he said I was smart to think about these things. I will be a better American.

"Then I pass the police station and I see black and white patrol cars and the patrolmen coming and going. I know they are protecting our city. My father says we pay taxes to pay these men. I think it's great. It makes me proud.

"Now when I go to the park and see the grass and flowers

and picnic tables I think, Why, we own this. I can stay there all day and have fun. We can have picnics and play ball. And because I think about owning all this I do not scatter papers or trash. I pick it up and put it in the boxes the park people set out for us to use.

"I think grownups should think about all this, too. I think we should think, My taxes pay for all this—the city hall, the courthouse, the state capitol and the national Capitol. Taxpayers everywhere help. They ought to be proud.

"I ride my bike in the bike lane along the street. I see the paved streets. I see the fire hydrants. I see the stop signs and the street work crews. I think, Isn't it wonderful? I am glad I am an American. I thank God for it.

"When I grow up I will try to make my country an even better country. I am starting now, because I think of it all as mine to take care of and enjoy. I am glad my teacher took us on the field day to Civic Center. It made me think of all this. Randall."

Lord, thank you for young minds, eager and idealistic. We thank you for their fresh insights and ambitions. Help the Randalls of our country keep their spirit of active participation in the working of the government, and keep them from being dismayed or disheartened by the frequently-expressed negative attitudes of other citizens. Inspire the young people and adults with high ideals for our country. Amen.

26

Emergency Run

With purpose of heart . . . cleave unto the Lord (Acts 11:23).

Endure hardness, as a good soldier of Jesus Christ (2 Tim. 2:3).

I was new on the escort duty I was performing at the Veterans Administration Hospital. The first week had been particularly difficult as I tried to learn the geography of the seemingly endless corridors. Someone had said there were five miles of corridors stretching over four floors. Though I always checked the posted directories, I often became lost while transporting a wheelchair patient from his unit to a laboratory. I needed to learn immediately the locations of Nuclear Medicine, Radiology, Blood Bank, Audiology, and so on.

My first real test came one afternoon about four o'clock, the between-shift time. Eileen, at the Escort Station phone, was scribbling out an order. She looked at me and said, "Here is an urgent run. They have a crisis in Emergency. They need blood. They're short of help. You are to go to the Blood Bank, then take the blood to Emergency. This run will put it all together for you."

My mind whirled. The enormity of it! Where is the Blood Bank? I'll get lost. They need the blood. I can't do this. I'm scared. I'm too inexperienced.

But something stopped these exploding thoughts. Forcibly I stilled myself by saying, "Think about God! You always do this in times of crisis."

That is what I did. In my mind I heard, "Peace. Be still. I am with you always."

As if God were already answering my prayer, I found the elevator waiting, doors ajar. I glanced at the directory. Blood Bank, fourth floor.

After walking a long corridor and making two turns, there it was. I pushed open the swinging doors and came into a sterile-looking room. It was my first glimpse of the Blood Bank, which was presided over by a doctor.

I was unconsciously expecting to just grab a bottle of blood and hurry to Emergency.

Not so. Without speaking, the doctor took my order sheet, checking it carefully against the one in front of him. He rechecked, even using a ruler to be certain he read the lines correctly.

"Hurry!" my thoughts cried.

But he did not. Deliberately he went to a large refrigerator.

He chose two bottles, checking and rechecking each label against the written request. One bottle contained a thick yellow fluid—plasma; the other, dark red fluids. This was Pack RBC—red blood cells, I had learned somewhere. Previously, by centrifugal force, the plasma and red blood cells had been separated.

The doctor brought the bottle to a nearby counter, placed the two bottles side by side between two plates, and connected them with narrow tubing. The plates began to squeeze the plastic bottles as he turned a switch. Soon the red and yellow joined, blended. There was whole red blood.

The doctor again checked one record against the other, while my thoughts said, "Hurry, hurry!"

He pushed a sheet before me for my signature, placed the bottles in a brown bag, and gave them to me. Precious cargo: life for a stranger. The swinging doors closed behind me. Now to Emergency. Could I find it without delay?

Again I forced myself to inner stillness. Again I prayed, "Guide me, and thank you."

Suddenly, a vast concept filled me. I was part of a trinity: donor, conveyor, and receiver. Somewhere in Emergency lay a patient, unknown to me, who needed my help, needed this precious blood for life.

My heart moved into a steady rhythm. I had complete confidence, knowing I was the link, tied to humanity in a way I had never known before. Communion with the supreme Being relaxes and strengthens us.

I reached Emergency without delay and more swinging doors closed behind me. A nurse was waiting. She took the package, pushed another paper in front of me for signing, then rushed into an inner room.

My mission completed successfully, I made my way back to the Escort Station. Yes, as Eileen had said, this run had put it all together for me. I had successfully fulfilled my task as the conveyor from donor to receiver.

Lord, we thank you for the days of growth in our lives, the days when we come to a sure knowledge of our place in your world, which is also our world. We are grateful for opportunities for the growth which comes through service to others. Thank you for giving us strength, courage, and calmness in times of urgent need. Amen.

27

When Charity and Gratitude Become Acquainted

As in water face answereth to face, so the heart of man to man (Prov. 27:19).

Be thou an example of the believers, in word, in conversation, in charity (1 Tim. 4:12).

Let us consider one another to provoke unto love and to good works (Heb. 10:24).

Withhold not good from them to whom it is due, when it is in the power of thine hand to do it (Prov. 3:27).

Let nothing be done through strife or vainglory; but in lowliness of mind let each esteem other better than themselves (Phil 2:3).

Mario, a seventeen-year-old high school exchange student from Italy, was speaking before an audience of teachers and parents. If any members of the audience had thought for a moment they were in for a boring half-hour listening to this youth speak to them, they soon found they were mistaken.

Dark-haired Mario, whose eagerness was scarcely concealed by his subdued manner, rose and bowed to his audience after a brief introduction by his school principal.

"First," Mario said, "I want to say thank you to America for allowing me the privilege of staying in your country as an exchange student. You will see why I say thank you after I have concluded this program. I have a little story to tell you. It's about charity and gratitude.

"But first let me say that nine months ago I did not know a word of English, except perhaps the word Coke." He smiled.

"The family I have lived with here in this country have been more than good to me. They have helped in every way to make my stay a happy one. My teachers have been good to me, too. I have tried hard, and I hope I have not failed those who put their trust in me. Now I want to show some slides of my native Milano and of Venice."

The projector in the center of the room began to hum, the lights dimmed, and pictures flickered on the screen beside Mario. He explained the historic buildings of his native Milano. When pictures of Venice, where people go by boat through the canals appeared, he explained about the city's sinking and how it would be impossible to collect the sum of money needed to save the city and its endangered treasures.

Mario talked slowly, with assurance, in a soft yet strong voice. Who in the audience did not have an increasing admiration for this young man who was doing his country a great justice by his intelligence, poise, and humility.

The slides part of the program ended and the lights came up. Mario was smiling in a mysterious way.

"Now," he said, "I want to thank you, I want to thank America for all it has done for me. I shall return home in a few weeks by way of your beautiful capital, Washington, D.C., and then on to the city known as the Big Apple . . ." Laughter and applause broke in, "New York.

"Now my story about charity and gratitude. Did you exercise charity when you permitted me to come here? Do I have gratitude in my heart? You could feel like do-gooders, you know. I could feel humiliated at accepting charity. So my story deals with charity and gratitude.

"Roman mythology tells it this way. Jupiter, the god supreme, invited all the dieties for a feast. Jupiter saw to it that his guests, the lesser dieties, had all the good things provided for their enjoyment. There was music, singing by a royal chorus, games, and a banquet.

"Jupiter, from his royal throne, watched the festivities with great pleasure. But then, not far from him, he chanced to see two beautiful goddesses sitting with their backs to each other, not saying a word. Nor did they seem to be enjoying the party.

"Jupiter descended from his throne and approached the goddesses. 'Since you two apparently do not know each other, let me introduce you,' he said. And that is what he did.

"Do you know who those two goddesses were? One was Charity; the other was Gratitude."

Mario paused, then went on. "You see, in my book, charity and gratitude are well-acquainted. I have accepted the charity of the education provided to me in your country. I have been grateful. I will always be grateful. When I return to my home in Milano I will be a better citizen because of my gratitude. I will help those less fortunate. But before I stop I want to tell you a secret." He smiled mischievously. "I believe your kindness to me was not charity at all. I believe it was given out of love, love from your big American hearts. And I thank you from my own heart!"

As one, the audience rose, and the applause was something Mario could not help but remember always. There were a few tear-streaked faces, too—something else he would remember.

Lord, point us to an awareness of the needs of others, and urge us to freely give of our talents and love. Reward us with the satisfaction of our sharing, and with our joyful acceptance of gratitude when it is expressed. Help us to not be disappointed if it is unexpressed, and to understand people as we continue to love them. Amen.

28

Don't Play in the Street

Let your light so shine before men, that they may see your good works, and glorify your Father which is in heaven (Matt. 5:16).

Be thou an example of the believers, in word, in conversation, in charity, in spirit, in faith, in purity (1 Tim. 4:12).

In all things shewing thyself a pattern of good works (Titus 2:7).

The little boys living in the Rockford Arms apartments constantly used forbidden territory—the street—for a makeshift baseball diamond.

The boys, ranging in years from eight to ten, had been

repeatedly warned not to play there by parents and by several patrol officers of the police department, who stopped their black and white squad cars and stepped out to interrupt tight games.

The policemen, singly or in pairs, strolled to what was purported to be center field. With much finger pointing, hand waving and loud warning, the officers delivered the law to the chronic misbehavers. "You are not to play in the street. It's against the law. You might get hit by a car. You might break windows."

The boys listened with respect to these symbols of the law, nodded a thousand promises, then scattered like startled birds.

Mission accomplished, the officers with satisfaction eased their purring vehicles around the corner. The boys, grinning, came out from hiding, picked up their mitts, bats, and balls to begin again their interrupted game.

The misbehavers continued misbehaving.

One afternoon, Mike, a well-known patrolman, came along in his black and white car. He parked carefully, a half block from the arena, got out, and walked casually to the makeshift diamond to watch the game in progress. True, the boys cast nervous glances at this tall, uniformed man. But they continued to play. True, the policeman was not ordering them off the street. But more pitchers made wild throws and more batters made wild strikes than usual. Was this a mild defiance of the law?

Mike continued to watch. He hooked his thumbs in his pockets and his side arm swung a bit energetically. Then he stepped to the spot serving as home plate and asked the pitcher, "May I see that ball?"

Mike carefully examined the awkwardly tossed ball. He spit on it and strolled to the pitcher's mound, a pile of sand. He shuffled his feet and kicked the sand. The batter at home plate readied his bat. Mike wound up and uncoiled his body like a professional. The batter missed.

Someone retrieved the ball from down the street, then

waited for a car to pass. A magic word, from Mike no doubt, ended the game. Mike, like the Pied Piper of Hamelin, led the group to the patrol car.

The boys stood about. They touched fenders, they examined tires. Mike opened the hood and pointed as he explained the intricacies of the engine and whatever else lies under the hood of a police car.

Now the boys piled into the car. They took turns sitting at the wheel. The police radio stuttered and stammered and was silent. The red signal light atop the car began to spin and blink. Finally, there was a blast from the siren.

The boys came out of the car. Mike slammed the door shut, leaned against it and with much gesturing talked to the boys. Was it about baseball or the police station? Or worse, jail?

When Mike opened the front and back doors the boys piled in again, but with Mike at the wheel. The car moved down the street, its souped-up engine purring like a jungle cat. A pretend trip to the city jail?

Soon the car reappeared. The boys tumbled out, laughing and clapping their hands. Mike waved to them as he drove away. While the car moved along, the boys followed, keeping hands on fenders as if begging Mike to stay. They waved long after he had disappeared.

The boys did not return to illegal playing in the street. They never did.

Why had Mike succeeded where others had failed?

Georgia, one mother, said, "For a short time Mike became one of the gang. And he knew secrets of childhood the other men did not know or did not choose to use. He knew youngsters are inquisitive. He shared his life and car with the boys. He gained their confidence. Mike shared himself with them. He was a good sport."

But there was still more.

A month later another mother reported excitedly, "Mike has done it again—something we parents should have done! Our church up the street has a vacant lot. Mike and the boys went to see if they could use the ground for baseball. They said they didn't want to play in the street. It wasn't safe." Mike's words?

It was arranged. Now the fathers referee, and Mike, on his afternoons off, plays with the boys. Those boys are proud. They know a cop, they play ball with a cop, and they say repeatedly, "Cops are great guys!"

Georgia says, "Mike is teacher, friend, leader. Our minister had a special Sunday dedicated to Mike. In his prayer he gave special thanks for men like Mike, men who take time to love others enough to help them."

Lord, open our eyes to the needs of others. Direct us to use the talents you gave us to satisfy needs of others as well as of ourselves. Amen.

29

Harrison's Short Successful Life

Thou shalt open thine hand wide unto thy brother (Deut. 15:11).

He stretched forth his hand toward his disciples, and said, Behold my mother and my brethren! (Matt. 12:49).

Strengthen thy brethren (Luke 22:32).

Harrison was dead.

The street where he had lived now seemed a haunted place. His mother and father sit behind closed doors, refusing to see even close friends. Only relatives gain admittance to the house where shades are drawn.

Everyone in the small town knew Harrison. They had known him all his eighteen years.

What did they know about Harrison?

"He was always so cheerful, polite, outgoing." That was Mrs. Orwell speaking.

His teachers said, "He never caused any trouble in school or around town. At home either, so his mother always said."

Harrison was always generous. He would stop to help a youngster with a broken bike. He helped sullen old Mr. Sykes with his lawn mower, and never seemed to mind that Mr. Sykes never thanked him.

Harrison graduated from high school with honors. He then attended junior college up on the hill, planning to become a space engineer. He and Jean, his best girl friend since early high-school days, planned to be married someday.

Yes, so far as anyone knew, Harrison had everything in his favor: a high IQ, friends, a good home. But one evening, while his parents were at prayer meeting, Harrison went to the garage, closed the door, and killed himself.

Killed himself! Why?

No doubt his parents, sitting in the suddenly darkened living room and silent house, ask themselves, "Why? Where did we go wrong? Did we hurt him in any way? How could we have? We had no problems, and we loved him."

Yet, Harrison had killed himself.

The whys went around town among friends and acquaintances. His girlfriend Jean, in near-collapse, cried, "Why, Harrison?"

The whys became more specific. "Did we ever take the time to praise him for his accomplishments, or did we just take him for granted? Did we . . . did we . . . ?" The self-questioning went on and on, around the town.

In time the self-questioning dwindled. But the people of the town did not forget. The tragedy had been too great.

Now the people's awareness of each other came into the atmosphere of the town. Everyone began to say, each in his own way, "We all loved Harrison, we admired him. But we never really told him, nor showed him our love and admiration. Maybe he never condemned us for that, but it left a hollow spot inside him. We must never show such neglect again."

Teachers began, unconsciously perhaps, to speak more gently and with greater understanding to their students. They showed greater understanding, too, of troubled children. Parents praised their children more and more for even small improvements.

Teenagers changed. Meeting a senior citizen carrying a heavy bag of groceries, a teenager often stopped, saying, "Let me help."

Mike, the mischievous boy living across the street from crabby Mrs. Thompson, said, "Mrs. Thompson, let me mow your lawn. I like to mow lawns. I won't charge you anything."

It was said later that Mrs. Thompson almost fainted. But she gave Mike a dollar, even though he first refused it.

Civic and church groups of the town became more aware of those who needed help. Who needed a pat on the shoulder? What could they do to improve their community?

All these changes were subtle. Harrison's name was not mentioned. But one Sunday morning Pastor Jones discussed it in a specially-prepared sermon, and summed it up with these words in his closing prayer. "Lord, through the death of Harrison we have become aware of the universal brotherhood of man and of the responsibility of reaching out and supporting each other. Help us to extend peaceful understanding to our neighbors, and to the world as we become more aware of other persons' needs. May we always remember to let the other one know we admire his accomplishments.

"Make us forgive, readily, touch our fellow men with love, give hope where it is needed, extend tenderness that heals secret troubled spots in the lives about us, spread joy rather than sadness, and be a source of strength to others.

"It took the short life of Harrison and its tragic end to bring us to our senses and to our responsibilities. May we always remember. Amen."

30

Whose Child Is This?

A man of understanding hath wisdom (Prov. 10:23).

First be reconciled to thy brother, and then come and offer thy gift (Matt. 5:24).

Be ye all of one mind, having compassion one of another, love as brethren (1 Peter 3:8).

Diane sat nervously in her chair. It would soon be her turn to speak. How would she, how could she, reveal her hurts and her guilt to the people sitting around the table in the church fellowship hall? But the purpose of this open counseling session was to reveal your problems and receive feedback from these sincere people who were also your friends.

Lacing her fingers together as if the very movement helped her to speak, she leaned forward.

"My mother said plaintively, 'Would you have been happier if you had been an orphan?'

"The question, so hurtful, came as a result of one of my outbursts. These outbursts came frequently, now that I was in the terrible-teens time of growth. 'You don't understand. You never understand. You want me to be what you want. I wish I had never been born!' I replied.

"I read in a psychology book that many parents are locked in their own private rooms of beliefs and routines. They have lost the key to the door, so they cannot understand why their children are way out there trying to build their own rooms of satisfaction without their parents."

Diane looked at her taut fingers, loosened them and then reached up with both hands to push her dark hair back from her face.

"Did my mother, I wonder, on my arrival into the world ask herself, 'Who in the world is this?' Did she think me a stranger from some distant and undiscovered world?

"I doubt it. My mother probably thought of me as an extension of herself, someone who would grow up dealing with the same problems she dealt with as a growing person, having the same hopes, the same dreams.

"As I grew my mother no doubt continued to ask herself 'Is this stranger mine?' I know I often asked myself, 'Is this my mother, really my mother? Or was some horrible mistake made at the hospital and I was given the wrong mother? She is so different from me. She doesn't understand me and never will.'

"But doesn't this terrible mistake seem to plague every parent—the difficulty of saying to the rebellious one, 'I don't understand you and what you want to do. But I love you. I want you to be happy.'

"My mother did not say that at all. Just the opposite. I continued to complain. 'You think I am selfish. I'm sorry, sorry.' I did not say what I wanted to say: 'It is you who are

99

selfish. If you were the Christian you believe yourself to be, you would try to understand.' No, I did not say it. Instead, I said, 'I am sorry. I don't know what makes me this way. I am stupid.'

"I'd rather throw the blame for her unhappiness on myself. and then feel guilty for not being what she wanted me to be, for not being a success according to her standards. This way I had the satisfaction, in a way, of feeling noble.

"Guilt! I still feel it. If my mother had called me her ex-daughter when I left home, it would have been easier. I would have felt sadness rather than guilt.

"And I am envious when I see rapport between a mother and her teenaged daughter, when the mother says, 'I chose my life. You are free to choose your life. I've tried to teach you as you grew so you could choose the constructive way. You have my prayers for your happiness.' A mother who can tell her child that is beautiful.

"Yes, the awful mistake made by most of us is that it is so difficult to be understanding. Certainly it is human for the parent to try to correct what he believes to be the mistakes of the child. But only by giving the child to himself can the parent expect to keep him."

Diane paused, hesitating to go on. "I know tonight most of you believe I've just talked about myself and a leftover sadness from my growing-up years. But that isn't the half of it. There's also my own daughter. She is saying the same things to me I said to my mother. I understand my mother now. I wish I could make myself say to my daughter, 'I'm sorry. I understand how you feel. I know I must let you go.' I pray, I turn the problem over to God, but then, I snatch the problem right back. I know I must let her go. How hard it is! I need your help, the help of all of you here tonight. I need your wisdom." Diane's head dropped to the table and she began to cry.

Lord, parents are stuck with their children, children are stuck with their parents. Often they have glaring differences of opinion. May we all, in dealing with others, whether they be family members, neighbors, or friends, deal with each other's differences with love and understanding. Constantly remind us that without charitable attitudes and acts love will be destroyed. Guide our love so that it allows the other person to grow in his own particular way in which he or she can live happily and productively. Amen.

31

The Policeman's Prayer

Judge not according to the appearance, but judge righteous judgment (John 7:24).

He that ruleth over men must be just (2 Sam. 23:3).

Let us consider one another to provoke unto love and to good works (Heb. 10:24).

I have a friend, Richard, in the state highway patrol, who told me about the following event in connection with his police work. He is still shaken by the discovery of the pattern his thinking had fallen into, and how changing it has affected his attitude toward his career.

Richard has been on the force five years. During this time he has, by his own ready admission, grown callouses on his mind and heart. And, really, who can blame him? In the course of his duties in the black and white patrol car, covering our section of Highway 15 to the county line, he has been in contact with all kinds of lawbreakers. He has been the object of violence more than once, and more than once has spent time in hospitals recovering from injuries received in the line of duty.

So it was perfectly natural for Richard to expect trouble the day he and his partner stopped to investigate a car parked on the shoulder immediately behind the on-off ramp.

Two teenagers, a boy and a girl, were seated in the car. Were they enjoying a joint? Popping pills? Experience had taught the officers it might be both. Richard took the left side of the car, his partner the right.

"Problems, Buddy?" Richard asked the boy, who looked up in surprise. Richard had his hand on his side arm, just in case.

The girl, sitting on the passenger side, replied before the boy had a chance. "Officer, Bob and I were late getting started on the way to my sister's home. We forgot to say our travelers' prayer. We're saying it now. Here it is." She offered a slip of paper.

Richard thought, "Now I've heard everything. A travelers' prayer!" He was accustomed to outrageous excuses.

"I'll have to ask you to get out of the car. Hands up," Richard ordered.

The teenagers, whitefaced with fear and anger, crawled from the car. While his partner covered the couple, Richard searched the car from front to back, side to side, and top to bottom.

He told me, "I was determined to pin something on those kids, whether there was something there or not. I found nothing."

Then he spotted the piece of paper the girl had offered to show him and picked it up.

Indeed, it was something called the travelers' prayer, and went something like this: Lord, as we set out on this journey, we ask your blessing. Guide and protect us so that we come to no harm. Let us in no way harm anyone we meet on the freeway and in the streets. Bless all those we meet today, and help us to be a blessing to them. Thank you for being near us. Amen.

Richard looked and looked at that paper. His body seemed to shrivel inside his smart-looking uniform.

The kids had told the truth. Richard said, "I judged them by a thousand others I'd been in contact with. I had begun to think there wasn't a clean one anywhere.

"Maybe it wasn't exactly according to our rules, but my partner and I apologized to the kids, and then we asked them to go with us to a fast food place just off the freeway. We bought them cokes, while we had coffees. The kids said they understood the search; we had a duty to do.

"But sometimes I lie awake nights, wondering. Did we damage two trusting hearts that day? I pray we didn't. Believe me, I hadn't prayed in a long time, but I've made up a prayer I say every day now when I start out. It's something that's become a part of me, even though I know I've got to be on the alert for trouble. That's part of my job. Here's the prayer. I think it could be fitting for all people.

"Dear Lord, as I go about my work today, let me not judge people by appearances. Let me know the facts before I pass judgment. Grant me the ability to be kind and understanding. The weak and the misguided need my help, the strong need a pat on the back. Take away from me all tendencies to prejudge, all inclinations to lump everyone I meet into one category. Amen."

32

What If Parents Had Never Met?

Honour thy father and thy mother (Exod. 20:12).

Behold, how good and how pleasant it is for brethren to dwell together in unity! (Ps. 133:1).

Ye have not chosen me, but I have chosen you, and ordained you, that ye should go and bring forth fruit (John 15:16).

Martha came in early one morning. Her eyes were wet. She had been crying, but now she was smiling and filled with gaiety. She held out a letter to me. "Read this," she said.

The letter was from her minister, a delightful person with

a great sense of humor. He had written it to Martha in honor of her eighty-eighth birthday.

"Martha, so pert, so spunky, so good for the world," the letter read. "Imagine how the world would fret if her folks had never met. How awful for the world to have been denied her presence. Congratulations and many, many more natal days!"

Martha said, "I was really feeling sorry for myself today. I was deep in pity, with my children being so far away. But this letter changed the day. I guess we all at some time wonder what we've been good for. We forget all the good things, especially when affairs aren't to our liking.

"I've made up a list of the what ifs the minister must have had in mind." Martha showed me the list, written in her precise hand.

"My husband, Jack, said I was the one woman in the world who could have made him as happy as I did. Oh," Martha laughed, "he doesn't know how many times I wanted to spout off at his crankiness. But I kept still and when he brought me strawberries instead of flowers, I loved him.

"I have two children who would not have been born if I hadn't loved him. Christine gave me two grandchildren. If my folks had never met, I'd not have been here to enjoy my children and grandchildren. And they'd not have been here to enjoy God's world. My husband and I would not have had the joy of knowing our love-produced children.

"Then, what pleasure to have known life, and to have all the satisfactions of finding niches for ourselves and being of service to others. I think of kindnesses given and kindnesses received. I remember the hours of volunteer work my friends and I put in at hospitals, how we worked in God's house, how we filled Christmas baskets for those less fortunate than we.

"And there has been my joy in nature, in sky and clouds, rain and snow, oceans and streams."

The what-if-our-parents-had-never-met list went on and on. Martha's heart and mind were running over with feelings of gratitude for having been born and for the gift of a long,

"This isn't about Einstein's theory of relativity," she said, laughing. "The incident I am about to relate was told to me by a friend who witnessed it. It's made me do much thinking about the relativity of our life views.

"A white woman and a black woman were sharing a mirror in the lounge of a department store. The white woman had just examined her reflection in the mirror, and said to herself, 'My, how pale I look today.'

"At the same time the black woman said, also to herself, 'My, I look pale today.'"

A white woman looking pale to herself, and a black woman saying the same about herself. It is a matter of relativity.

"What about other relativities in life? Understanding them, at least being aware of them, certainly brings us to a more Christian attitude toward our fellowmen," Roberta told her audience.

"The refugee from a war-disrupted country is grateful to have reached the safety of a peaceful, friendly country. He may have lost all his possessions, but he gives thanks to God for shelter—any kind of shelter. He no doubt is thankful for food, though it may at first taste strange to him. However, the native of the host country who has never been without life's essentials may have nothing good to say about his life or his homeland.

"The person with an amputated leg is grateful for the artificial limb that enables him to be ambulatory once again, while the person next to him grumbles because the lesion on his foot has not healed as rapidly as the doctor had predicted."

Roberta told about the people who spend their lives on houseboats in Hong Kong Harbor. Some of them are born on the boats and live there until they die, going ashore only occasionally. On the boats they maintain their homes, raise their families, keep their pets, perhaps make their livings and transact their businesses. Have we any doubt these people are grateful for the good that is theirs, for might not the alternatives be worse? Do they not give God thanks?

And what about the people living on the hilltops in their mansions? Are they happy and content? Or have they found that wealth does not guarantee happiness?

We begin to think further about it. Is there not misery, is there not happiness—pockets of both—all over the world? And might not the person who appears to be deprived find peace and contentment and reliance on God, while the apparently successful person may be miserable and alienated from God?

Roberta paused before returning her audience's minds to their own country.

"Consider the man traveling to and from work in a sagging-fendered car. Returning home after a long hard day, he is smiling, even whistling. But how could he be happy in that old car?"

"We consider it. Perhaps he was out of work for some time, but now has a good job and can provide for his family. Whatever his lot in life may be, the car gets him where he needs and wants to go. His joy does not depend on the car's cosmetic condition.

"We here in this room," Roberta continued, "see each other from various perspectives. We may differ in our opinions, in our appreciation of life's blessings, but the differing does not make either of us wrong. We may all be right. We all have sustenance to continue living; however, some of us require more necessities or luxuries, some fewer, in order to live happy, creative lives.

"Think again of the white woman and the black woman in the lounge. Each thought herself to be looking pale that day. But, it's all a matter of relativities, isn't it?"

Lord, give us understanding of other persons, whether they be relatives, friends, neighbors, or complete strangers. Help us to allow the other people with whom we share this world to live the best ways in which they can find their own happiness. But also make us always ready to give any possible assistance to a person in need, and to do it with love. Amen.

useful, and happy life. For both of us, the minister's suggestion led to our awareness of endless blessings in our lives, all because our parents had given birth to us.

As she left for home, Martha saluted the heavens. "Thanks, parents, for having met!" she said.

Lord, with gratitude we remember our parents and their love which produced us. Give us the desires and opportunities in which to express this thankfulness in service to others. We thank you for your protection and loving care in all ways. We thank you that we can care for each other through love. Amen.

33

Relativities

A wise man will hear, and will increase learning; and a man of understanding shall attain unto wise counsels (Prov. 1:5).

By works a man is justified, and not by faith only (James 2:24).

Thou hast been faithful over a few things, I will make you ruler over many things (Matt. 25:23).

Whatsoever things are true, whatsoever things are honest, whatsoever things are just . . . think on these things (Phil. 4:8).

Roberta, the guest speaker at Thursday's Let's Think Club, gave her audience much to think about.

34

Is Your Slogan "IAK?"

Behold, how good and how pleasant it is for brethren to dwell together in unity! (Ps. 133:1).

Guide our feet into the way of peace (Luke 1:79).

Foolish and unlearned questions avoid, knowing that they do gender strifes (2 Tim. 2:23).

There is a story of a certain man meeting a friend on the street. The friend was wearing a sign suspended from his neck. The sign read, "IAK."

"What do those letters mean?" asked the first man.

"They stand for, 'I am confused,'" replied the second man.

"But confused begins with a c."

"That shows you how confused I am!"

Who isn't confused at times? Sometimes we become so confused we panic, and are frozen into immobility. Confusion arises in all areas of life.

One religious denomination teaches one doctrine, another teaches another. We are brought up to believe still another. The more we study and think about it, the more confused and, perhaps, disturbed we become.

The child hears his father tell him not to do this or that. Then the child sees his father doing the same thing he told his son not to do. The child is confused, disturbed.

At school the teacher pronounces a word one way, but the child has heard his parents pronounce it differently. More confusion.

We are told the sky is falling, then we hear it isn't. No wonder we might easily spell confusion with a k.

A minister solved a growing and increasingly disturbing problem in his church. He delivered a special sermon. One of his impressive statements was this: "Under all conditions I am profoundly undisturbed."

He went on to explain, "No matter what, I know the sky will not fall. These building walls will not come tumbling down. There is a peaceful solution to the problems facing our church at this present time. First, we must deliver ourselves into our heavenly Father's care."

As the sermon progressed, heads began to nod affirmatively. Attitudes began to change. Soon some members began to say to their opponents, "I see your point."

A settling-down period began. One man said, "Perhaps no one is exactly right. Let's get together on this, take what we think is the best from each side's opinion, and put the two together."

Before long the disagreements were forgotten, or, if not completely forgotten, then lived with peaceably.

Children, too, need to take part in the calming process. A teacher in an elementary-school class was having a hard day. Nothing went right. Everyone was about to give up because of the confusion. One child said, "I'll be glad when I can get home so I can chew some celery. That always settles me down."

The alert teacher remarked, "Do you think your teacher goes home in a peaceful and quiet mood after a day like this?"

Jennie broke in, "I'll just be glad to get home and go to my room and shut the door, I'm so confused!"

"Don't add to the confusion," said Rick. "Let the teacher talk!"

"Yes," continued the teacher, smiling. "Like Chicken Little, I often think the sky is falling. But I go home to what I call my peaceful island. My cat, Jinx, is always waiting for me. He purrs, and just the sound takes away some of the confusion about what I might or might not have done wrong that day. I sit down and say a prayer."

"What do you say in your prayer?" asked a child.

"I tell God I am thankful I have a good mind, a mind I use to try to make our days in school happier and to help all of you to learn. Then I thank God for my food and my home. Some days my prayers are short; on others they're longer."

"The long ones come after days like this," said Mike, and everyone laughed.

The teacher continued, "Finally, the confusion in my mind goes away. God takes it away."

"Aren't you thankful you have us?" asked Jimmie, wistfully.

"It must be pretty hard to be thankful for us on days like this," George answered for his teacher.

Another child added, "But if we didn't have any problems to work out, we'd probably never learn much. When you solve a problem it makes you feel good."

"Yes," said the teacher "we do have to have problems in order to grow. But we get confused if we go round and round looking for answers rather than sitting down, thinking calmly, and asking for God's help."

The minister's statement, "Under all conditions, I am profoundly undisturbed," is a worthy slogan to supersede "IAK."

Lord, give us islands of peace in which to settle our sometimes-churning minds so that, with your constant help, we are able to solve our own problems and possibly others'. Help us to be able to see the other person's point of view and to achieve the harmonious relationships in which people find open doors to your guidance for their lives. Amen.

35

Jean's Upside-down Life

It is not for you to know the times or the seasons, which the Father hath put in his own power (Acts 1:7).

Now we see through a glass, darkly; but then face to face: now I know in part; but then I shall know even as also I am known (1 Cor. 13:12).

After Jean finished school and was on her own, she began what she called her "delicious living alone time." In her large family, no one could ever be alone, and now Jean gloried in this new, refreshing freedom. Daytimes she was busy at work and with people, but evenings were her very own. She could have guests, or not have guests. She soon found her life tied by the neat little bows of a schedule:

breakfast at the same time each day, dinner, TV news, some beautiful friends.

Then Bob entered her life. What happened? Her neat little bows became untied and even raveled. Nothing was the same. Dinners were anytime from seven to eleven. Calls were, "I'll pick you up in an hour, or a half-hour."

Jean thought, "Must I have my clothes hanging from the ceiling, ready for action? All I'll have to do is pull the cord and presto! They'll drop on me. Instant dressing!"

But she loved Bob and gradually forgot about the neat little schedule bows that had tied up her life. Jean and Bob married and the bows disappeared. There was no trace of the rigid schedule she'd once enjoyed.

Jean and Bob moved every two years. Jean would think more and more of the roots of her life—friends, church, volunteer work, her garden. When she started to feel at home, permanent, what would happen? Why, they'd move again, of course.

Jean began to think she was living an upside-down life. While each move was in process, she grieved for her friends she had made over the two years. She missed the house she had barely finished redecorating, the garden she had worked in. Finally, however, she settled down, planned the redecorating of the new house, went to church, joined in the activities, and made new friends.

In one place Jean became acquainted with Air Force wives. Those gallant women never complained about frequent transfers, not even her new friend Anne, whose husband was in "classified" and was heaven-knew-where in the world. Anne calmly tended her children and her house, and took part in community activities.

"Did these Air Force wives have some special secret imparted to them by the base commander?" Jean wondered. She dared not ask, however, lest she receive the curt response, "That's classified."

So Jean went on fussing and fuming, even while putting down fresh roots which would, in two years, be pulled up. But eventually Jean learned something, not from people, but from a plant.

In the mail one day she received a catalogue from a nursery which grew epiphyllums. Epiphyllums, or orchid cacti, Jean read, are extremely odd plants. They have no leaves. Rather, their thick triangular stems are green and serve as their leaves. The lovely shining flowers burst forth directly from the stems. What is further startling about these plants is that they grow whether they are planted right side up or upside down. They have no right side up. Life's force is so strong in them they don't care what position they find themselves in.

"What about me?" Jean thought. Hadn't she learned to adapt to each place she had lived? All these years, every time she moved, she had thought she was in some kind of trouble by having no roots. What time she had wasted resenting the moves.

But now she realized life had sprung from her no matter how upside down her circumstances had seemed. Without being fully aware of it, she had had the courage, the interest, and the ambition to build a new life and bring forth flowers.

"And who has been responsible for my doing all this?" Jean asked herself. Why, God had been her silent partner. Only God had not been fussing and fuming. God had seen to it she got busy. God, the great creative Spirit, had daily filled her with the energy and ambition to put down new roots. How much more she could have accomplished, Jean told herself, if she had been serene and confident as she grew, like the orchid cactus, whether or not she was upside down.

Lord, we know you are our companion. Our roots are deep in your goodness and eternal spirit. Our own vitality is nurtured by you, whether we feel we are living our lives right side up or upside down. We are always grateful for your caring and your understanding. Amen.